IN THE DAYS OF
QUEEN VICTORIA

IN THE DAYS OF QUEEN VICTORIA

BY

EVA MARCH TAPPAN

ILLUSTRATED FROM FAMOUS PAINTINGS AND ENGRAVINGS

YESTERDAY'S CLASSICS

CHAPEL HILL, NORTH CAROLINA

Cover and arrangement © 2007 Yesterday's Classics.

This edition, first published in 2007 by Yesterday's Classics, is an unabridged republication of the work originally published by Hutchinson & Co. in 1905. For a listing of the books published by Yesterday's Classics, please visit www.yesterdaysclassics.com. Yesterday's Classics is the publishing arm of the Baldwin Project which presents the complete text of dozens of classic books for children at www.mainlesson.com under the editorship of Lisa M. Ripperton and T. A. Roth.

ISBN-10: 1-59915-038-7

ISBN-13: 978-1-59915-038-3

Yesterday's Classics
PO Box 3418
Chapel Hill, NC 27515

PREFACE

To her own people Queen Victoria was England itself, the emblem of the realm and of the empire. To millions who were not her people the words "the Queen" always brought to thought the well-beloved woman who for nearly sixty-four years wore the crown of Great Britain and gave freely to her country of the gift that was in her.

Other women have been controlled by devotion to duty, other women have been moved to action by readiness of sympathy, but few have united so harmoniously a strong determination to do the right with a never-failing gentleness, a childlike sympathy with unyielding strength of purpose.

Happy is the realm that can count on the list of its sovereigns one whose career was so strongly marked by unfaltering faithfulness, by honesty of aim, and by statesmanlike wisdom of action.

EVA MARCH TAPPAN

CONTENTS

		Page
I.	BABY DRINA	1
II.	THE SCHOOLDAYS OF A PRINCESS	16
III.	EXAMINATION DAY	32
IV.	A QUEEN AT EIGHTEEN	50
V.	THE CORONATION	65
VI.	THE COMING OF THE PRINCE	84
VII.	HOUSEKEEPING IN A PALACE	103
VIII.	A HOME OF OUR OWN	122
IX.	NIS! NIS! NIS! HURRAH!	138
X.	THE ROYAL YOUNG PEOPLE	158
XI.	THE QUEEN IN SORROW	174
XII.	THE LITTLE FOLK	191
XIII.	MOTHER AND EMPRESS	205
XIV.	THE JUBILEE SEASON	220
XV.	THE QUEEN AND THE CHILDREN	235
XVI.	THE CLOSING YEARS	249

CHAPTER I

BABY DRINA

"ELIZABETH would be a good name for her," said the Duke of Kent. "Elizabeth was the greatest woman who ever sat on the throne of England. The English people are used to the name, and they like it."

"But would the Emperor Alexander be pleased?" asked the Duchess. "If he is to be godfather, ought she not to be named for him?"

"Alexandra—no; Alexandrina," said the Duke thoughtfully. "Perhaps you are right. 'Queen Alexandrina' has a good sound, and the day may come when the sovereign of England will be as glad of the friendship of the Emperor of Russia as the Regent is to-day."

"Are you so sure, Edward, that she will be a sovereign?" asked his wife with a smile.

"Doesn't she look like a queen?" demanded the Duke. "Look at her golden hair and her blue eyes! There, see how she put her hand out, just as if she was giving a command! I don't believe any baby a week old ever did that before. The next time I review the troops she shall go with me. You're a soldier's daughter, little one. Come and see the world that you are to conquer." He lifted the tiny baby, much to the displeasure of the nurse, and carried her across the room to the window that looked out upon Kensington Garden. "Now, little one," he whispered into the baby's ear, "they don't believe us and we won't talk about it, but you'll be queen some day."

"Is that the way every father behaves with his first baby?" asked the Duchess.

"They're much alike, your Grace," replied the nurse rather grimly, as she followed the Duke to the window with a blanket on her arm. The Duke was accustomed to commanding thousands of men, and every one of them trembled if his weapons and uniform were not spotless, or if he had been guilty of the least neglect of duty. In more than one battle the Duke had stood so firmly that he had received the thanks of Parliament for his bravery and fearlessness. He would never have surrendered a city to a besieging army, but now he had met his match, and he laid the baby in the nurse's arms with the utmost meekness.

The question of a name for the child was not yet decided, for the wishes of someone else had to be considered, and that was the Prince Regent, the Duke's older brother, George. He thought it proper that his niece should be named Georgiana in honor of himself.

"Georgiana let it be," said the Duke of Kent, "her first name shall be Alexandrina."

"Then Georgiana it shall *not* be," declared the Prince Regent. "No niece of mine shall put my name second to any king or emperor here in my own country. Call her Alexandrina Alexandra Alexander, if you choose, but she'll not be called Alexandrina Georgiana."

When the time for the christening had arrived the Archbishop of Canterbury and the Bishop of London came to Kensington in company with the crimson velvet curtains from the chapel at St. James' and a beautiful golden font which had been taken from the Tower for the baptism of the royal baby. The Archbishop and the Bishop, the Prince Regent, and another brother of the Duke of Kent, who was to represent the Emperor of Russia as godfather, all stood around the golden font in the magnificent cupola room, the grand saloon of Kensington Palace. The godmothers were the child's grandmother and aunt, and they were represented by English princesses. All the royal family were present.

After the prayers had been said and the promises of the sponsors made, the Archbishop took the little Princess in his arms and, turning to the godfathers and the godmothers, he said: "Name this child."

"Alexandrina," responded the Duke of York.

"Give her another name," bade the Duke of Kent in a low tone.

"Name her for her mother, then," said the Prince Regent to the Archbishop, and the baby was christened Alexandrina Victoria.

It made little difference to either the Duke or the baby how the Prince Regent might feel about her name, for the Duke was the happiest of fathers, and the little Drina, as the Princess was called, was a merry, sweet-tempered baby. Everyone at Kensington loved her, and over the sea was grandmother, the Dowager Duchess of Coburg, who could hardly wait for the day to come when she would be able to see the child. "How pretty the little Mayflower will be," she wrote, "when I see it in a year's time." Another letter said: "The English like queens, and the niece of the beloved Princess Charlotte will be most dear to them." Princess Charlotte was the only child of Prince George, and the nation had loved her and longed to have her for their queen. She had married Leopold, the brother of the Duchess of Kent, and had died only two years before "Princess Drina" was born.

The succession to the English crown was in a peculiar condition. The king, George III., had become insane, and his eldest son, George, was ruling as Prince Regent. If the Regent lived longer than his father, he would become George IV. His next younger brother was Frederick, Duke of York; then came William, Duke of Clarence; and then the Duke of Kent. George and Frederick had no children, and William's baby girl died on the very day that the Princess Alexandrina was born. If these three brothers died without children, the Duke of Kent would become king; but even then, if the Duke should have a son, the law was that he, rather than the daughter, should inherit the crown. The baby Princess, then, stood fifth in the succession to the throne, and a child born to any one of these three uncles, or a son born to her father, would remove her still further from sovereignty.

The English people had talked of all these possibilities. The Duke of Kent had also several younger brothers, but they were all middle-aged men, the youngest forty-five, and not one of them had a child. If all the children of George III. died without heirs, the English crown would descend to a line of Germans who had never walked on English soil. "We have had one king who could not speak English," said the people, "and we do not want another." The Duke of Kent was a general favorite among them, and they hoped that he, and after him his daughter, would become their ruler. Indeed, they hoped for this so strongly that they began to feel sure that it would come to pass. Everyone wanted to see the little Princess. Many a person lingered under the palace windows for hours, and went away feeling well repaid for the delay if he had caught a glimpse of the royal baby in her nurse's arms.

When the Princess was four months old, the Duke gave orders one afternoon that she should be made ready for a drive with him.

"But is it not the day of the military review on Hounslow Heath?" asked the Duchess.

"Yes," replied the Duke, "and where else should a soldier's daughter be but at a review? I want to see how she likes the army. You know she will be at the head of the army some day," he added half in jest and half in earnest. "Won't you let me have her?" The Duchess shook her head playfully. Just then the nurse entered the room with the little Princess in her outdoor wraps. The tall Duke caught up the child and ran to the carriage like a naughty boy with a forbidden plaything, and the nurse followed.

At the review the Duke was not so stern a disciplinarian as usual, for more than one man who was expected to stand "eyes front" took a sly look at the pretty baby in her nurse's arms, and the proud father forgot to blame him for the misdemeanor. After the review the people gathered about the carriage.

"God bless the child," cried an old man. "She'll be a Princess Charlotte to us."

"Look at her sweet face," said another. "Did you ever see such bright blue eyes? She'll be a queen who can see what her people want."

There were hurrahs for the Princess and hurrahs for the Duke. Then a voice in the crowd cried: "Give us a rousing cheer for the Duchess who cares for her own baby and doesn't leave her to the hired folk."

In all this hubbub and confusion the blue-eyed baby did not cry or show the least fear. "She's a soldier's child," said the Duke with delight, and he took her from the nurse and helped her to wave her tiny hand to the admiring crowd.

Prince George had never been on good terms with his brother, the Duke of Kent, and after the affair of the name he was less friendly than ever. He was always jealous of the child, and when he heard of her reception at the review he was thoroughly angry. "That infant is too young to be brought into public," he declared.

BABY DRINA

She was not brought into so public a place again, but she won friends wherever she went. The Duke could not bear to have her away from him for an hour, and the greatest honor he could show to a guest was to allow him to take the little one in his arms. An old friend was at the Palace, one evening, and when he rose to go, the Duke said: "No, come with me first and see the child in her crib." As they entered the room of the little Princess, the Duke said: "We are going to Sidmouth in two or three days to cheat the winter, and so we may not meet again for some time. I want you to give my child your blessing. Pray for her, not merely that her life may be brilliant and free from trouble, but that God will bless her, and that in all the years to come He will guide her and guard her." The prayer was made, and the Duke responded with an earnest "Amen."

In a few days the family set out for Sidmouth. Kensington was becoming cold and damp, and the precious baby must not be risked in the London chills of the late autumn. The Duchess, moreover, had devoted herself so closely to her child that she needed a change and rest.

At Sidmouth the old happy life of the past six months went on for a little while. The house was so small that it was called "hardly more than a cottage," but it had pretty verandas and bay windows, shaded by climbing roses and honeysuckles. It stood on a sunny knoll, with tall trees circling around it. Just below the knoll was a little brook running merrily to the sea, a quarter of a mile away, and, following the lead of the brook, was the road. Sidmouth was a nest of sunbeams, and the baby Princess was well and strong. "She is too healthy, I fear," wrote the Duke, "in the opinion of some members of my family by whom she is regarded as an intruder."

The people of Sidmouth did not look upon the pretty, blue-eyed baby as an intruder, and there was great excitement in the village when it was known that the Duke had taken Woolbrook Glen. Every boy in the country around was eager to see the soldier Duke who had been in real battles, and every girl longed for a sight of the little Princess. There was no difficulty in seeing them when they had once come, for whenever it was pleasant they were out of doors, walking or driving. A lady who met the party one morning wrote that the Duke and the Duchess were strolling along arm in arm, and close to them was the nurse carrying the Princess with her white swansdown bonnet and cloak. She was holding out her hand to the Duke, and just as the village people drew near, he took her from the nurse and lifted her to his shoulder.

When the Duke had been away from the house, his first thought on returning was the little daughter. One morning, only a few days after this meeting with the lady and her children, he took a long walk in the rain. He was hardly over the threshold on his return before he called, "Where's my daughter? Bring little Drina."

"But, Edward," the Duchess objected, "your boots must be wet through. Won't you change them first? You will surely be ill."

BABY DRINA

"Soldiers aren't ill, my lady," replied the Duke, laughing. "I never was ill in all my life. Where's my queen?"

An hour's romp with the merry baby followed. But then came a chill, and the strong man was overcome with inflammation of the lungs. In those days physicians had little knowledge how to treat such a disease. They had an idea that whenever one was feverish he had too much blood, and that some of it must be taken away; so the Duke was bled until, if he had not been in the least ill, the loss of blood would have made him faint and weak. A messenger was sent to London to bring a famous doctor, but when he came the Duke was dead. "I could have done nothing else," said the great man, "except to bleed him much more than you have done."

Prince Leopold had come to Sidmouth a day or two earlier, and he went with the Duchess and the Princess to London. The villagers gathered about the carriage to bid a silent farewell to the sorrowful company. Many of them were weeping, and their tears flowed still faster when the nurse held the baby up to the carriage window and whispered, "Say good-by to the people;" for the little one waved her hand and patted the glass and sprang up and down in her nurse's arms without the least realization of her loss.

The carriage rolled away, but the people stood watching it until it was out of sight.

"That's the sweetest child in all England," said one woman, wiping her eyes with the corner of her apron, "and now the poor little thing will have no father."

"Did ever you see a man so fond of his child as the Duke?" said another with a sob.

"King George had nine sons," said a man who stood near, "and the Duke was every whit the best of them. The King never treated him fairly. When the others wanted money, they had it; but when the Duke needed it, his father just said, 'Get along as you can.' There wasn't one of the sons that the King wasn't kinder to than to the Duke."

"He'll have little more chance to be kind or unkind," declared another. "Have you not heard the news from London? The King is very ill, and the Prince Regent will soon be George IV."

"It's bad luck speaking ill of him that's to be king," said one, "but the man that's gone to London in his coffin was the man that I'd have liked to see on the throne."

"Will the Duchess go back to her own land, think you?" questioned the first woman.

"Yes, that she will," replied the second positively. "There never was a woman that loved her own people better than she. Folks say she writes her mother every day of her life."

"I say she'll not go back," declared one of the men with equal positiveness. "She'll do her duty, and her duty is to care for the Princess. God bless her, and make her our queen some day."

BABY DRINA

So the people in the village talked, and so people were talking throughout the kingdom. After the first sad days were past the question had to be decided by the Duchess and her devoted brother Leopold. The Duchess loved her family and her old home at Amorbach, near Heidelberg. There she and the Duke had spent the first months of their married life, and nothing would have helped her more to bear her loneliness than a return to the Bavarian Palace, in which every room was associated with memories of him. She was a stranger in England and she could not even speak the language of the country. The Duke's sisters loved her, and Adelaide, who had been a German princess before she became the wife of the Duke of Clarence, gave her the warmest sympathy in this time of sorrow; but the Regent disliked her and had always seemed indignant at the possibility that his brother's child would inherit the throne. The Regent had now become king, for his father had died on the very day of the Duchess's return to London. Unless a child was born to either the Duke of York or the Duke of Clarence, the baby Princess would become queen at their death. The child who would rule England ought to be brought up in England.

There was something else to be considered, however. When the Duchess was only a girl of seventeen she had become the wife of the Prince of Leiningen, and at his death he had made her sole guardian of their two children, Charles and Féodore. As soon as Charles was old enough he would succeed his father as ruler of Leiningen, but until then his mother was Regent.

"Is it right for me to neglect my duties in Bavaria?" questioned the Duchess; "to give up the regency of Leiningen? Shall I neglect Charles to care for Drina's interest?"

"Charles will be well cared for," said Prince Leopold. "His people love him already and will be true to him. England is a great kingdom. It is not an easy land to rule. A queen who has grown up in another country will never hold the hearts of the people."

"True," said the Duchess. "I must live in England. That is my duty to my child and to her country."

How the Duchess and her child were to live was a question of much importance. The King could not refuse to allow them to occupy their old apartments in Kensington Palace, but the Duchess was almost penniless. Nearly all the money which her first husband had left her she had been obliged to give up on her second marriage, and she had surrendered all the Duke's property to his creditors to go as far as it would in paying his debts. Some money had been settled upon her when she married the Duke, but that was so tied up that it would be many months before she could touch it. The only plea that she could make to the King would be on the ground that her child might become his heir, and nothing would have enraged him so much as to suggest such a thing. Whatever Parliament might appropriate to the Princess would be given against the wishes of the King, and there would, at any rate, be a long delay. It was a strange condition of affairs. The child would probably have millions at her command before many years had passed, but for the present there was no money even to pay the wages of the servants for their care of her.

If this story had been a fairy tale, the fairy godmother with the magic wand would have been called upon to shower golden guineas into the empty purse, but in this case it was the good uncle who came to the aid of his Princess niece. When Prince Leopold married the Princess Charlotte he went to England to live, for he expected that some day his wife would become Queen of Great Britain. After her death he made his home in England, but spent much of his time in travelling. He was not rich, but he was glad to help his sister as much as possible, and after the death of the Duke of Kent he made her and her children his first care.

It was decided, then, that the Duchess would remain in England, and that Kensington Palace should become the home of the Princess Alexandrina Victoria. This was a large, comfortable-looking abode. It had been a favorite home of several of the English sovereigns. About it were gardens cut into beds shaped like scrolls, palm leaves, ovals, circles, and all sorts of conventional figures so prim and stiff that one might well have wondered how flowers ever dared to grow in any shape but rectangular. The yew trees were trimmed into peacocks and lions and other kinds of birds and beasts. All this was interesting only as a curiosity, but there was a pretty pond and there were long, beautiful avenues of trees. There were flowers and shrubs and soft green turf. It was out of the fog and smoke of the city; indeed it was so far out that there was danger of robbers to the man who ventured to walk or drive at night through the unlighted roads. For many years after the birth of the Princess a bell was rung Sunday evenings so that all Londoners might meet and guard against danger by going over the lonely way to their homes in one large company.

The life at Kensington was very quiet. No one would have guessed from seeing the royal baby that the fate which lay before her was different from that to be expected for any other child who was not the daughter of a Prince. She spent much of the time out of doors, at first in the arms of her nurse, then in a tiny carriage, in which her half-sister, the Princess Féodore, liked to draw her about. "She must learn never to be afraid of people," declared the wise mother, and before the child could speak plainly she was taught to make a little bow when strangers came near her carriage and say, "Morning, lady," or "Morning, sir."

The little girl was happy, but life was hard for the mother. She had given up her home and her friends, and now she had to give up even her own language, for English and not German must be her child's mother tongue, and she set to work bravely to conquer the mysteries of English. Her greatest comfort in her loneliness was the company of the Duchess Adelaide, wife of the Duke of Clarence. For many weeks after the death of the Duke of Kent, the Duchess drove to Kensington every day to spend some time with her sister-in-law. When the Princess was about a year and a half old, a little daughter was born to the Duchess Adelaide, but in three months she was again childless. She had none of the royal brothers' jealousy of the baby at Kensington, and she wrote to the Duchess of

Kent, "My little girls are dead, but your child lives, and she shall be mine, too."

CHAPTER II

THE SCHOOLDAYS OF A PRINCESS

NOTHING could be more simple than the order of the Princess' day at Kensington. Breakfast was at eight, and it was eaten out of doors whenever the weather was good. The Princess sat in a tiny rosewood chair beside her mother, and the little girl's breakfast was spread on a low table before her. Whatever other children might have, there were no luxuries for this child. Bread and milk and fruit made up her breakfast, and nothing more would have been given her no matter how she might have begged for it. After breakfast she would have liked to play with her beloved Féodore, but Féodore had to go to her lessons. When the weather was fair, however, a pleasure awaited the little girl. Her uncle, the Duke of York, had given her a white donkey, and at this hour she was allowed to ride it in Kensington Gardens. Her nurse walked beside her, and on the other side was an old soldier whom her father had especially liked. This riding was a great delight to the child, but there was sometimes a storm of childish wrath before the hour was over, for the Duchess had said, "She must ride

THE SCHOOLDAYS OF A PRINCESS

and walk by turns," and when the turn came for walking, the tiny maiden often objected to obeying her mother's orders.

When it was time for the Duchess to eat luncheon, the Princess had her dinner, but it was so simple a meal that many of the servants of the palace would have felt themselves very hardly used if they had had no greater variety and no richer fare. The afternoon was often spent under the trees, and at some time, either before supper or after, came a drive with her mother. Supper was at seven, but the little girl's meal consisted of nothing but bread and milk. At nine o'clock she was put to bed, not in the nursery, but in her mother's room, for the Duchess had no idea of being separated from her children, and the Princess Féodore slept at one side of her mother, while on the other hand stood the little bed of the baby sister.

It was a simple, happy, healthy life. The great objection to it was that the child rarely had a playmate of her own age. Two little girls, daughters of an old friend of the Duke's, came once a week to see her, but they were several years her seniors. Féodore was never weary of playing with her, but Féodore was almost twelve years older, so that when the child was four years old, Féodore was quite a young lady. Perhaps no one realized how much she needed children of her own age, for she was so merry and cheerful, so ready to be pleased and amused, and so friendly with everyone who came near her.

A learned clergyman reported that when he called on the Duchess the little Princess was on the

IN THE DAYS OF QUEEN VICTORIA

floor beside her mother with her playthings, "of which I soon became one," he added.

One day the Duchess said: "Drina, there is a little girl only a year older than you who plays wonderfully well on the harp. Should you like to hear her?"

"I'm almost four years old," was the child's reply. "What is her name?"

"She is called Lyra," said the Duchess. "Should you like to hear her play?"

The Princess was very fond of music even when she was hardly more than a baby, and she could scarcely wait for the day to come when she could hear the little girl. At last Lyra and her harp were brought to the palace, and the music began. The talented child played piece after piece, then she stopped a moment to rest. This was the Princess' opportunity. Music was good, but a real little girl was a great rarity, and the small hostess began a conversation.

"Does your doll have a red dress?" she asked. "Mine has, and she has a bonnet with swansdown on it. Does yours have a bonnet?"

"I haven't any doll," answered Lyra.

"Haven't you any playroom?" asked the Princess wonderingly.

"No," said the little musician.

The Princess had supposed that all children had dolls and toys, and she said: "I have a playroom upstairs, and there are dolls in it and a house for them and a big, big ship like the one my papa sailed in once. Haven't you any ship or any doll-house?"

"No."

"Haven't you any sister Féodore?"

"No."

Then the warm-hearted little Princess threw her arm around the child musician and said:

"Come over here to the rug, and let's play. You shall have some of my playthings, and perhaps your mamma will make you a doll-house when you go home."

The Duchess had left the two children for a few minutes, and when she returned they were sitting on the fur rug in front of the fire. The harp was forgotten, and they were having a delightful time playing dolls, just as if they were not the one a princess and the other a musical prodigy. They were too busy to notice the Duchess, and as she stood at the door a moment, she heard her little daughter saying:

"You may have the doll to take home with you, Lyra. Put on her red dress and her white bonnet and her cloak, for she'll be ill if you don't. Her name is Adelaide, for that is my aunt's name."

The Princess was not yet four years old, but her mother was beginning to feel somewhat anxious about her education. Other children might play, but the child who was to be queen of England must not be allowed to give even her babyhood to amusement. The mother began to teach her the alphabet, but the little girl had a very decided will of her own, and she did not wish to learn the alphabet.

"But you will never be able to read books as I do, if you do not learn," said the mother.

"Then I'll learn," promised the child. "I'll learn very quick."

The alphabet was learned, but the resolutions of three-year old children do not always endure, and the small student objected to further study.

"My little girl does not like her books as well as I could wish," wrote the Duchess to her mother; but the grandmother took the part of the child. "Do not tease your little puss with learning," was her reply. "She is so young still. Albert is only making eyes at a picture book." This Albert was one of the Princess' German cousins, only a few weeks younger than she; and the great delight of the Coburg grandmother was to compare the growth and attainments of the two children and note all their amusing little speeches.

The Duchess, however, did not follow the advice of her mother, but more than a month before her little daughter was four years old she decided to engage a tutor for her. She herself and Féodore were reading English with the Rev. Mr. Davys, the clergyman of a neighboring parish, and during even the first few lessons the Duchess was so charmed with his gentle, kindly manner and his intellectual ability that she said to him one day: "You teach so well that I wish you would teach my little daughter."

So it was that the learned clergyman appeared at the palace one bright April morning armed with a box of alphabet blocks. The Duchess seemed quite troubled and anxious about the small child's intellectual deficiencies, and when the preparations for the lesson had been made, she said:

"Now, Victoria, if you are good and say your lesson well, I will give you the box of bright-colored straw that you wanted."

"I'll be good, mamma," the little girl promised, "but won't you please give me the box first?"

The lesson began with a review of the alphabet; then came a struggle with the mysterious *b-a, b-e, b-i, b-o, b-u, b-y,* "which we did not quite conquer," the tutor regretfully writes. Mr. Davys kept a journal of the progress of the Princess during the first two years of his instruction, and he records gravely after the second lesson that she pronounced *much* as *muts*, that he did not succeed in teaching her to count as far as five, and that when he tried to show her how to make an *o*, he could not make her move her hand in the right direction. It seems to have been a somewhat willful little hand, for a week later when he wished her to make an *h*, she would make nothing but *o's*. "If you will make *h* to-day," said the patient tutor, "you shall have a copy of *o's* to-morrow;" but when to-morrow had come and the copy had been prepared, the capricious little maiden did not care to make *o*, she preferred to make *h*.

The troubled instructor tried various plans to interest his small charge. He wrote short words on cards and asked her to bring them to him from another part of the room as he named them. He read her stories and nursery rhymes, and one day, when he seems to have been almost at his wit's end, he persuaded the Princess Féodore and her governess to stand with his little pupil and recite as if they were in a class at school. His report for that day records with a good deal of satisfaction, "This seemed to please her." Willful as she was, however, she was very tender-hearted, and when he asked her to spell the word *bad*, she sobbed and cried, because she fancied that he was applying it to herself.

When Mr. Davys came in the morning, he would frequently inquire if she had been good. One day he asked the Duchess:

"Was the Princess good while she was in the nursery?"

"She was good this morning," replied her mother, "but yesterday there was quite a little storm."

"Yes, mamma," added the honest little girl, "there were two storms, one when I was washed and another when I was dressed."

Sometimes her honesty put her mother into a difficult position. One day the Duchess said:

"Victoria, when you are naughty you make both me and yourself very unhappy."

"No, mamma," the child replied, "not me, but you."

The lessons went on with much regularity, considering that the pupil was a princess. On her fourth birthday she not only had a birthday party, but she was invited to court. "Uncle King," as she called George IV., gave a state dinner, and she was asked to be one of the guests. Most children, however, would have thought the invitation hardly worth accepting, for she was only brought into the room for a few minutes to speak to the King and the royal family, then she was taken away to eat her usual simple meal.

When the Princess had been studying with Mr. Davys about five months, she was taken to the seashore, and from there she wrote, or, rather, printed, a letter to her tutor. It said:

"MY DEAR SIR I DO NOT FORGET MY LETTERS NOR WILL I FORGET YOU VICTORIA."

The name Alexandrina had been gradually dropped. The Duchess had feared at first that as "Victoria" was unfamiliar in England, the English people might dislike it. Moreover, as the royal brothers were so unfriendly to her, she did not wish that the use of her name should prejudice them against the child. There was little danger of anyone disliking the child, however, for she was so winsome a young maiden that whoever spoke to her became her friend. One of her most devoted admirers was her Uncle Leopold, and her idea of the highest bliss was to make a visit at his house. A few months after the beginning of her education, she visited him, and Mr. Davys drove to the house twice a week to continue her instruction. Her uncle was present at the lessons, and he was as troubled as the Duchess because little Victoria did not like to read.

It is no wonder that the child enjoyed her visits to Claremont. Prince Leopold's home was a large brick mansion, with stately cedars on the lawn, and high up on a column a great bronze peacock that was a source of wonder and amusement. There was a lake, with groves of pines beyond it. There was a farm, with lambs and calves and ducklings. Best of all, there was Uncle Leopold, who was always ready to walk or drive with her, and to tell her wonderful stories.

It was very delightful to visit an uncle who was a prince, but even at Claremont it was never forgotten that the wee child was being trained to be a queen. The stories must not be without a moral; her uncle's charming talks of flowers and animals must be planned to introduce her to botany and natural history; and even in her play she was carefully watched lest some thoughtlessness should be overlooked which ought to be checked. One day she took her tiny rake and began to make a haycock, but before it was done something else interested her, and she dropped the rake. "No, no, Princess," called her governess, "come back and finish the haycock. You must never leave a thing half done."

In Kensington she was never taken to church, lest she should attract too much attention, but service was read in the chapel of the palace. At Claremont, however, she went to the village church. She usually wore a white dress, made as simply as that of any village child, and a plain little straw bonnet; but at the

THE SCHOOLDAYS OF A PRINCESS

church door the resemblance ended, for while other children might fidget about or perhaps go to sleep, the Princess had some hard work to do. Mr. Davys had said that she was "volatile," and disliked fixing her attention. That fault must be corrected, of course, and so the child was required to remember and repeat to her mother not only the text but the principal heads of the sermon, no matter how uninteresting it might be. The little girl must have longed to do something, somewhere, with no one to watch her. There is a story that when she once went to visit the Duchess of Clarence, her aunt asked: "Now, Victoria, what should you like to do? What will be the greatest treat I can give you?" and, the little child replied, "Oh, Aunt Adelaide, if you will only let me clean the windows, I'd rather do that than anything else."

Money matters had become somewhat easier for the Duchess, as an allowance had been made her which enabled her to give the Princess such surroundings and advantages as ought to be given to one in her position. Nevertheless, the simplicity of the child's daily life was not altered, and her pocket money was not made any more lavish. When the little girl was seven years old, she was taken to a bazaar, where she bought presents for one after another until she had reached the bottom of her rather shallow purse. But there was a half-crown box that she did so want to give to someone!

"I should like this very much," she said wistfully, "but I have no more money to-day."

"That makes no difference," replied the storekeeper, and he began to wrap the box with her other purchases.

"No," objected the governess, "the Princess has not the money, and she must not buy what she cannot pay for."

"Then I will lay it aside until she can purchase it," said the storekeeper, and the little girl exclaimed, "Oh, thank you! if you will be so good."

When the day for the payment of her allowance came, the child did not delay a moment, but long before her breakfast hour she appeared at the store to pay for the box and carry it home with her. She was not at all afraid of carrying bundles, and thought it was a delightful expedition to go to the milliner's with her mother and Féodore to buy a new hat, to wait in the shop until it was trimmed, and then carry it home in her own hand.

The great excitement of her seventh year was the visit that she paid the King. Disagreeable as he often was to the mother, he made himself quite charming to the child, and he was delighted with the frank affection that she showed him in return.

"The band shall play whatever you choose," he said to her. "What shall it be?"

"I should like 'God Save the King,' " replied the little girl.

It was hard to be jealous of such an heir to the throne as that. During her stay the King had taken her to drive, and this was a great event, for he himself had held the reins. When she was saying farewell at the close of the three days' visit, he asked, "What have you enjoyed most during your visit?" and he was much pleased when she answered, "Oh, Uncle King, the drive I had with you." It is no wonder that the grandmother in Coburg wrote, "The little monkey must have pleased and amused him; she is such a pretty, clever child."

The Duchess was beginning to receive the reward that she deserved for giving up her home and her friends, not only in the result of her devotion to her little daughter as shown in the child's character, but also in the appreciation of herself and her efforts which was felt in her adopted country. In both the House of Lords and the House of Commons speeches had been made paying the warmest tributes to the manner in which she was bringing up the little girl who was to become the queen.

Before Victoria was eight years old, it was thought to be time for her education to receive still more attention, though one would suppose that there need have been no anxiety about the intellectual progress of the child, who before she was six years old could repeat the heads of one of the lengthy sermons of the day. Mr. Davys was now formally appointed her tutor, and he went to live at Kensington. Then, indeed, there was work. Miss Lehzen, governess of the Princess Féodore, taught the child as usual; a writing-master made his appearance, who taught her the clear, refined, and dignified hand that never changed; a teacher of singing was engaged; another teacher instructed her in dancing; a Royal Academician taught her drawing; German and French were also studied.

Mr. Davys' special work was to teach her history and English, and the number of books that she read with him is somewhat startling. During the year 1826 there were four books of Scriptural stories and four books of moral stories on her list. The children's books of the day had a fashion of not being satisfied with teaching one thing at a time, and even one of the four natural histories that she read contrived to make the story of each bird contain some profound moral instruction. One book on English history and one on modern history in general appear on the list. Geography and grammar are each represented by two small volumes. Poetry appears in the form of "The Infant's Minstrel," a title which the eight-year old child of to-day would utterly scorn. "General Knowledge" is represented by one book on the famous picture galleries, castles, and other noteworthy structures in England, and another describing the occupations and trades of the land. Even here, however, moral lessons had their allotted place, and each trade was made to teach some moral truth. The third book of the series described the quaint old customs of the kingdom.

During the following three years the instruction of the Princess was continued on similar lines. In 1827, the year in which her eighth birthday occurred, she began a book with the comprehensive title, "An Introduction to Astronomy, Geography, and the Use of the Globes." After she had studied this book with the hard name for two years, it seems a great intellectual downfall to find her "promoted" to "Elements of Geography for the Use of Young Children." In 1828 she began Latin. She also studied the catechism and then an abridgment of the two Testaments. Remembering that the little girl was studying French, German, music, dancing, and drawing, one wonders how she ever "crowded it in." Fortunately, her schedule for the week has been preserved, and it is interesting reading. Her day's work began at half-past nine. On Monday morning the first hour was given to geography and natural history, the second to a drawing lesson. From half-past eleven till three was devoted to dinner and either playing or walking. From three to four she drew or wrote a Latin exercise. The following hour was given to French, and from five to six came music and "repetition"—whatever that may have been—for Mr. Davys. After her three hours of study in the afternoon, without even a ten-minutes' "recess," the day's work was at an end, and from six to nine there was no more studying; but there seems to have been some instructive reading aloud by either the Duchess or Miss Lehzen, for the story has survived that when the Duchess was reading Roman history and read the old story of Cornelia's pointing to her sons and declaring, "These are my jewels," the small critic remarked, "But, mamma, she ought to have said, 'These are my carnelians.' "

No two days in the Princess' week were alike. One hour a week was devoted to learning the catechism, another to a dancing lesson, another to needlework and learning poetry by heart. All this teaching went on for six days in the week, for she had no Saturday holidays; and on Saturday morning came an hour that would alarm most children, for it was devoted to a repetition to Mr. Davys of all that she had learned during the week. Her lessons were made as interesting as possible by explanations and stories and pictures and games. A history and a little German grammar were written expressly for her; but, after all, the little girl was the one who had to do the work. She had to understand and learn and remember, and even if she was a princess, no one could do these things for her. Sir Walter Scott dined with the Duchess of Kent during Victoria's ninth year. He wrote in his journal: "Was presented to the little Princess Victoria, the heir-apparent to the throne as things now stand." It is no wonder that he added, "This lady is educated with much care."

The same year stole away the beloved Féodore, for she married a German prince and went to the Continent to live. This was a great loss to the little Princess, for she was so carefully guarded that Féodore had been almost her only playmate. Other children had companions without number; they went to children's parties and had good times generally; but a party was a great rarity in the life of the Princess, and she was ten years old before she went to a children's ball.

This famous ball which she then attended was her first sight of a court ceremonial. It was given in honor of a little girl of her own age, Maria, Queen of Portugal, who was making a visit to England. The Princess wore a simple white dress, but the little Donna Maria was gorgeous in crimson velvet all ablaze with jewels. Every one was comparing the two children in dress and looks and manners. The plain dress of the Princess was generally preferred, and her graceful

THE SCHOOLDAYS OF A PRINCESS

manners were admired, but the Portuguese queen was called the prettier. When the King first talked of giving this ball, a lady of the court exclaimed, "Oh, do! It will be so nice to see the *two little queens* dancing together." The King was very angry at the speech, but he finally decided to give the ball, and the "two little queens" did dance in the same quadrille. It is rather sad to relate that the small lady from Portugal fell down and hurt herself, and, in spite of the sympathy of the King, she went away crying, while the English Princess danced on and had the most delightful evening of her life. Then Cinderella went to bed, and in the morning she awoke to the workaday world that she had left for a single evening.

CHAPTER III

EXAMINATION DAY

WHEN Queen Victoria was a tiny child, she is said to have asked her mother one day, "Mamma, why is it that when Féodore and I are walking all the gentlemen raise their hats to me and not to her?" In 1830, when she was nearly eleven years old, her mother and her teachers thought that it was time for her question to be answered. The King was so ill that everyone knew he could not live many months. The Duke of York had died three years earlier; therefore at the King's death William, Duke of Clarence, would ascend the throne, and Victoria would succeed him.

It seems quite probable that the bright little girl had before this time answered the question for herself. There are stories that if she failed in a lesson a certain teasing boy cousin of hers used to say, "Yes, a pretty queen you will make!" and then he would suggest that when a queen did not rule well her head was likely to be cut off. Another story is that when the child was reading aloud to her mother about the Princess Charlotte, she suddenly looked up from her book and asked, "Mamma, shall I ever be a queen?" Tradition

EXAMINATION DAY

says that the Duchess replied: "It is very possible. I want you to be a good woman, and then you will be a good queen." Whether there is any truth in these stories or not, the child was too observing not to have noticed when very young that she was treated differently from other children, even her sister Féodore. She lived very simply, and Miss Lehzen was always at hand to correct the least approach to a fault; but she could not have failed to see that she was watched wherever she went and that far more attention was paid to her than to her mother. Indeed, she herself said long afterwards that the knowledge of her position came to her gradually and that she "cried much" at the thought of ever having to be a queen.

The little girl kept these thoughts to herself, and even her mother did not know that she was dreading a future on a throne. There are several accounts of just how she was finally told that she would some day wear the crown, but a version which may be trusted comes from Mr. Davys.

"Princess," he said, "to-morrow I wish you to give me a chart of the kings and queens of England."

When morning came, she gave him the chart, and he read it carefully. Then he said:

"It is well done, but it does not go far enough. You have put down 'Uncle King' as reigning, and you have written 'Uncle William' as the heir to the throne, but who should follow him?"

The little girl hesitated, then she said, "I hardly liked to put down myself."

IN THE DAYS OF QUEEN VICTORIA

One story of the way the announcement was made to the Princess was written—nearly forty years after the event—by her strict and adoring governess, but it makes her out such a priggish, Pharisaical little moralizer that one cannot help fancying that the devoted woman unconsciously put into the mouth of her idol the speeches that seemed to her appropriate, not to the child, but to the occasion. She says that when the Princess was told of her position, she declared: "Many a child would boast, but they don't know the difficulty. There is much splendor, but there is more responsibility." Then the governess reminded her that if her Aunt Adelaide should have children they would be the ones to ascend the throne. According to this account, the child answered: "If it were so, I should be very glad, for I know by the love Aunt Adelaide bears me how fond she is of children." It seems probable that after the Princess had been told what lay before her, Miss Lehzen made speeches somewhat like these, and that the conscientious, tender-hearted little girl assented to them.

Mr. Davys told the Duchess about the chart, and she wrote at once to the Bishop of London that the Princess now understood her position. The letter ended, "We have everything to hope from this child."

It must have given the little girl of eleven years a strange feeling to read a chart of sovereigns of her country and know that her own name would be written in the next vacant place. She had seen the deference paid to "Uncle King," she knew that his will was law, and it must have made the child's brain whirl to think "Some day I shall be in his place." She had al-

EXAMINATION DAY

ways been trained to the most strict obedience, but she knew that some day whatever order she chose to give would be obeyed. She seems to have thought more of the responsibility of the throne than of its glories; but if she had felt ever so much inclined to boast, she would soon have realized that after all she was only a little girl who must obey rather than command, for the first consequence of her queenly prospects was an examination in her lessons before two learned bishops.

The Duchess believed that the training of the future queen was the most important matter in the country. She could hardly have helped feeling that she had been most successful in her efforts to make the child what she ought to be, but after all, she herself was a German, her child was to rule an English realm, and the careful mother wished to make sure that the little girl was having the kind of instruction that would best prepare her for the difficult position she would have to fill. She selected two bishops as her advisers, men of much learning and fine character, and wrote them a long letter about the Princess. She told them what masters had been chosen for her and in what branch each one had instructed her. She enclosed a list of the books the Princess had read, a record of every lesson she had taken, and the schedule of her study hours. She said that she herself had been present at almost every lesson, and that Miss Lehzen, whose special task it was to assist the little girl in preparing her work for the different masters, was always in attendance.

With this letter went a report from each instructor, stating not only what books she had used but what his opinion was of her progress and ability. Although there was so much temptation to use flattery, these reports seem to have been written with remarkable sincerity and truthfulness. The writing master said that his pupil had "a peculiar talent" for arithmetic, but he was apparently not quite satisfied with her handwriting, for he closed with the sentence, "If the Princess endeavors to imitate her writing examples, her success is certain." The teacher of German wrote, "Her orthography is now tolerably correct," but he did not show the least enthusiasm over his statement, "There is no doubt of her knowing the leading rules of the German language quite well," though surely this was no small acquisition for a child of eleven. The French teacher declared that her pronunciation was perfect, that she was well advanced in knowledge of French grammar and could carry on a conversation in French, but that she spoke better than she wrote. He added: "The Princess is much further advanced than is usually the case with children of her age." Mr. Davys, with his great love for his little pupil, seems to have had a struggle with himself to keep from speaking of her as warmly as he longed to speak, but he did allow himself to say at the close of his report:

"It is my expectation that the disposition and attainments of the Princess will be such as to gratify the anxious wishes, as well as to reward the earnest exertions, with which your Royal Highness has watched over the education of the Princess."

These honest, straightforward reports were sent to the two bishops. The Duchess asked them to read the papers carefully and then examine the "singularly

EXAMINATION DAY

situated child," as she called the Princess, to see whether she had made as much progress as she should have done, and in what respects they would suggest any change of method and teaching.

Three weeks after the letter was written the two bishops went to Kensington and examined the little maiden in "Scripture, catechism, English history, Latin, and arithmetic." Both were gentle, kindly men, and both had little children of their own. Evidently they knew how to question the royal child in such a fashion that she was not startled or made too nervous to do her best, for one of them wrote in his journal about the examination, "The result was very satisfactory." The bishops went home from Kensington, and three days later they sent the anxious mother a report of the interview. They wrote that they had asked the Princess "a great variety of questions," and that her answers showed she had learned "with the understanding as well as with the memory." They were so well pleased with the results of their visit, they said, that they had no change to recommend in the course which had been pursued. So it was that the little girl began her public life, not by congratulations and entertainments and rejoicings, but by a thorough examination in her studies before two learned men.

Two months after the bishops' visit to Kensington the Princess passed her eleventh birthday. One month later "Uncle King" died, and "Uncle William" became sovereign, with the title of William IV. At William's death Victoria would become queen, and as that event might occur before she was eighteen and capable of ruling for herself, it was necessary to have a guardian appointed at once, so that, if it should come to pass, there would be no delay in matters of state.

A law was proposed in Parliament called the Regency Bill. As it was possible that William would have a child, Victoria was spoken of as the "heir presumptive"—that is, the one who is presumed or expected to be the heir, although with a possibility of changes that would put someone else before her. The bill provided that if she should come to the crown before she was eighteen, her mother should be her guardian and should rule the country in her name until she was of age. This bill became a law, and few laws have been so pleasing to both houses of Parliament and to the whole country. Speeches were made by prominent statesmen praising the Duchess of Kent and her manner of training her little daughter. The grandmother in Coburg wrote, "May God bless and protect our little darling," and the whole country echoed the prayer.

When Parliament was prorogued, or closed until the next session, the Princess was with her Aunt Adelaide, who was now the Queen. They stood together at one of the palace windows watching the procession, while the people shouted, "Hurrah for Queen Adelaide! Long live the Queen!" Then the loving aunt took the little girl by the hand and led her out on the balcony so that all might see her. The people cheered louder than before, not only for the Princess, but for the generous woman who had not a thought of jealousy because it was the child of her friend and not one of her own little girls that stood by her side.

EXAMINATION DAY

King William was fond of the child, but he did not like the mother. The Duchess always spoke of him with respect and kindness, but she contrived to have her own way in bringing up her daughter, and she was so quick-witted that she could usually prove, though in a most courteous and deferential manner, that he was in the wrong. He was very indignant that Victoria was not allowed to spend time at court, but there was nothing for him to say when the mother quietly took the ground that the little girl was not strong enough for the excitements of court life. Soon after his accession he sent the Prime Minister to the Duchess to express his opinion that the education of the heir presumptive ought to be in charge of some clergyman of high rank in the church, and not in that of the minister of a little country parish. The Duchess replied with the utmost courtesy. "Convey to his Majesty my gratitude," she said to the Prime Minister, "for the interest that he has manifested. Say to him that I agree with him perfectly that the education of the Princess ought to be intrusted to a dignitary of the church." Then she added: "I have every ground for being satisfied with Mr. Davys, and I think there can be no reason why he should not be placed in as high a position as his Majesty could wish." King William must have raged when he received the message, but he was helpless, and there was really nothing to do but to follow the suggestion of the Duchess. This was done, and Mr. Davys became Dean of Chester.

One other official was, however, added to the household of the Princess, a "state governess," the Duchess of Northumberland. Her business was to attend the royal child on all state occasions and to teach her the details of court etiquette that were to be observed. This lady had nothing to do with the education of the Princess in any other respect, and Miss Lehzen remained her governess as before.

Miss Lehzen, or Baroness Lehzen, for King George had made her a German baroness, was a finely educated woman, the daughter of a German clergyman. She had come to England with the Duchess of Kent as governess to the Princess Féodore, and she had performed her duties so satisfactorily that the Duchess was glad to be able to place the Princess Victoria in her charge. She was a woman of keen, sagacious judgment, with the ability to see everything that was going on about her, and not at all afraid to express her opinions. One day when an aide-de-camp of one of the royal dukes was presented to her, she greeted him with the frank speech: "I can see that you are not a fop or a dandy, as most of your Guardsmen are." She was severe in her manner, but her bluntest speeches were made with such a friendly glance of her shrewd and kindly eyes that most people who met her became, like the aide-de-camp, her loyal friends. Many years later her former pupil said of her: "I adored her, though I was greatly in awe of her. She really seemed to have no thought but for me."

The education of the schoolgirl Princess went on in much the same way as during the previous years. Her study hours were observed with such strictness that even when a favored guest at Kensington was about to take his departure, she was not allowed to leave her work for a moment to say good-by. Occa-

EXAMINATION DAY

sionally, however, an interruption came, and three months before she was twelve years of age the books had to be closed for one day that she might make her first appearance at Queen Adelaide's drawing room. She wore a white dress, hardly more elaborate than her ordinary gowns, but a diamond ornament was in her hair, and around her neck was a string of pearls. She stood beside the Queen, and although the ceremonies were almost as unwonted to her as they would have been to any other child of her age, she did not appear embarrassed, but seemed to enjoy her new experience. Baroness Lehzen wrote a letter to a friend about this time describing the little girl. She said:

"My Princess will be twelve years old tomorrow. She is not tall, but very pretty; has dark blue eyes, and a mouth which, though not tiny, is very good-tempered and pleasant; very fine teeth, a small but graceful figure, and a very small foot. Her whole bearing is so childish and engaging that one could not desire a more amiable child." The Baroness seems to have just returned from some absence when she wrote the letter, for she adds, "She was dressed to receive me in white muslin, with a coral necklace."

During this year, 1831, while the glories of Victoria's brilliant future were beginning to shine faintly about her, the first sorrows of her life came to her in the death of her grandmother of Coburg and the departure of her Uncle Leopold for Belgium. The year before, he had been asked to become king of Greece, but had refused. Now the throne of Belgium was offered him, and he accepted it. The happiest days of the little niece had been spent with him, and the child, who, in spite of her royal birth, had so few pleasures, was sadly grieved at his departure. All her life he had been her devoted friend, always near, and always ready to do anything to please her. Child as she was, she knew enough of thrones and sovereigns to understand that the visits of kings and queens must be few and far between, and that she could never again have the delightful times of her earlier years.

The coronation of King William took place in September, but neither the Duchess nor the Princess was present. No one knew the reason of their absence, and, therefore, all sorts of stories were spread abroad. "The Princess is not strong enough to attend so long and wearisome a ceremonial," said one. "Her mother keeps her away to spite the King," declared another; and yet another reason assigned—and this was probably the true one—was that the Princess was not allowed to go because the King had refused to give her the place in the procession which her rank and position demanded.

Whatever reason may have been the correct one, the Princess remained at home, but she did some little traveling during the summer. It was only around the western part of the Isle of Wight, but to the child whose journeys until the previous season had been hardly more than from Kensington to London or to Claremont these little trips were full of interest.

The following summer brought much more of travel. Not only the King but the people of the kingdom in general were beginning to feel somewhat aggrieved that so little was seen of the Princess. The

EXAMINATION DAY

The Princess Victoria and her Mother,
the Duchess of Kent 1834—*From a drawing
by Sir George Hayter.*

Duchess believed that the best way for the future Queen to know her realm was to see it, and that the best way to win the loyalty of her future subjects was for them to see her. She thought that her daughter was now old enough to enjoy and appreciate journeys through the country. These journeys were not lengthy, for the travelers did not leave England except for a short stay at Anglesey, but they could hardly fail to be of interest to a wide-awake girl of thirteen who wanted to "see things and know things."

The general course of their travel was from Kensington to the northwest, and its limit was the little island of Anglesey. Of course the child who had not been allowed to leave a haycock unfinished lest she should develop a tendency to leave things incomplete was not permitted to make an expedition like this without a vast amount of instruction. She was required to keep a journal, and she was seldom allowed to look upon the manufacture of any article without listening to an explanation of the process. It speaks well for her intelligence and her wish to learn that she seems to have been genuinely interested in these explanations. She found a tiny model of a cotton loom as fascinating as most children would find a new toy, and she was never weary of watching the manufacture of nails. As a memento of the visit to the nail-makers she carried away with the greatest delight a little gold box that they had presented to her. Within the box was a quill, and in the quill was a vast number of nails of all varieties, but so tiny that they could hardly be seen without a magnifying glass. Other gifts were made her. At the University Press she was presented with a richly bound

EXAMINATION DAY

Bible and a piece of white satin, on which was printed a glowing account of her visit. Here in Oxford she was enthusiastic in her enjoyment of the Bodleian Library. One thing in this library interested her especially, a book of Latin exercises in which Queen Elizabeth wrote when she was thirteen, just the age of the Princess. Of course the little visitor compared her own handwriting with that of Elizabeth, and the thought must have passed through her mind that some day her exercises and copybooks would perhaps be put into libraries to be looked at as she was looking at Queen Elizabeth's.

Other events than receiving gifts and studying manufactures came into those weeks of travel. The Princess laid the corner stone of a boys' school; she planted a little oak tree on the estate of one of her entertainers; in Anglesey she presented the prizes at the National Eisteddfod, a musical and literary festival which had been celebrated annually from ancient times; she listened to addresses without number from mayors and vice chancellors, and she was present at the formal opening of the new bridge over the Dee, which for this reason was named the Victoria Bridge. One thing which seems to have made a special impression upon the child's mind, and which she noted particularly in her journal, was that she was allowed to dine with her mother and the guests at seven o'clock.

Traveling in those days was quite a different matter from making a journey to-day. One or two short railroads had been built in England, but it was many years too early for the comfortable, rapid express trains of the present time, and the journeys of the

Princess were made entirely by carriage. She had set off for Kensington with a little company of attendants, very few, indeed, considering her position as heir presumptive, but it was hardly possible, without offending the loyal people of the places through which they passed, to refuse the honors which were shown to her and her mother and the requests of the yeomanry of various counties that begged the privilege of escorting them. In the days of Queen Elizabeth, that lover of gorgeousness used to make journeys about her kingdom that were regarded as an excuse for all magnificence and lavishness. These were called progresses, and now King William often jested about "little Victoria's royal progresses." He was not exactly pleased, however, and he kept a somewhat jealous watch of the honors that were paid to her.

The next year the Princess and her mother spent considerable time in their yacht, and the King had a fresh cause of annoyance in the fact that now they were greeted not only with addresses but with the firing of guns. He could not endure that anyone but himself should receive the royal salutes. "The thing is not legal," he said to the naval authorities. "Stop those poppings." The naval authorities respectfully insisted that the thing *was* legal. The King had not learned wisdom from his previous encounters with the Duchess of Kent, and in his dilemma he actually tried to compel her to refuse to accept the salutes. The dignified lady replied with all courtesy: "If the King wishes to offer me a slight in the face of the people, he can offer it so easily that he should not ask me to make the task easier." King William was fairly worsted, but he

EXAMINATION DAY

would not yield. He called the Privy Council and ordered them to pass an order that even the royal flag should not be saluted unless the vessel flying it bore either the King or the Queen.

To turn from royal salutes and mayors' addresses and the laying of corner stones to playing with dolls is a little startling, but such was the course of the Princess' life. She was heir to the throne, and she could bestow prizes and receive delegations and meet the eager gaze of thousands without being at all troubled or embarrassed, but she was a child for all that; she was not allowed to sit at the table when her mother gave an elaborate dinner party for the King, and she still retained her liking for the dolls that her lack of playmates had made so dear to her. There is now in existence a little copybook on which is written "List of my dolls." By their number and their interest, they certainly deserve the honor of being catalogued, even at the present time, for there were 132 of them, and they were often dressed to imitate noted persons of the day. Most of them were little wooden creatures from three to nine inches high, with sharply pointed noses, cheeks red as a cherry in some one spot—wherever the brush of the maker had chanced to hit—jet black hair, and the most convenient joints, that enabled the small bodies to be arranged in many attitudes. The men dolls had small black mustaches, and the women dolls were distinguished by little yellow "back-combs" painted on the black dab which represented their hair. The baby dolls were made of rags, upon which comical little faces were painted.

IN THE DAYS OF QUEEN VICTORIA

The fascination of these dolls does not lie in their beauty, but in their wardrobes. Most of them were dressed between 1831 and 1833, or when the Princess was from twelve to fourteen years old. One group represents the play of Kenilworth, which she had evidently seen. The Earl of Leicester is gorgeous in knee-breeches of pink satin, with slashes of white silk. His tunic reverses the order and is of white satin slashed with pink. He wears the blue ribbon of the Order of the Garter and a wide black velvet hat swept with yellow and white plumes. Queen Elizabeth appears in cloth of gold with enormous puffed sleeves. From her shoulders hangs a long train lined with bright crimson plush and trimmed with ermine. She wears crimson plush shoes and a heavy girdle of gold beads.

There are all sorts of characters among these little wooden people. There are court ladies, actors, and dandified young gallants. Perched on a table is a merry little ballet-dancer in blue satin trimmed with pink and yellow roses. There are mothers with their babies, and there is "Mrs. Martha," a buxom housekeeper, with a white lawn frock, full sleeves, and purple apron pinked all around. She wears a white lace cap adorned with many frills and tied under her small wooden chin with pink ribbons. She stands beside a home-made dressing table of cardboard covered with white brocade.

The conscientious little owner of these dolls marked carefully which ones she herself dressed and in which she was helped by the Baroness Lehzen. The wardrobes of thirty-two were made entirely by the fingers of the little girl, and, remembering the schedule of

EXAMINATION DAY

studies, it is a wonder how she found the time; one hopes that at least the hour marked "Needlework and learning poetry by heart" was sometimes devoted to this purpose, though how any dressmaker, old or young, could learn poetry with a court costume on her hands is a mystery.

It is equally a mystery how even the most skillful of childish fingers could manufacture such tiny ruffles and finish two-inch aprons with microscopic pockets whereon were almost invisible bows. Handkerchiefs half an inch square have drawn borders and are embroidered with colored silk initials. Little knitted stockings beautify the pointed wooden feet; bead bracelets adorn the funny little wooden arms that hang from the short sleeves; coronets and crowns and wreaths glorify the small wooden heads.

The Princess had a long board full of pegs into which the feet of these little favorites of hers fitted, and here she rehearsed dramas and operas and pantomimes. Even in her play with dolls, however she could not be entirely free from the burden of her destiny, for sometimes they were used by the state governess to explain court ceremonials and teach the etiquette of various occasions. When the Princess was fully fourteen, the dolls were packed away, though no one guessed how soon the little owner would be called upon to decide, not the color of a doll's gown, but the fate of men and women and the weighty questions of a nation.

CHAPTER IV

A QUEEN AT EIGHTEEN

D URING the years from 1833 to Victoria's eighteenth birthday, on May 24, 1837, her life was sometimes that of a child, sometimes that of a young woman. Much of the time she lived quietly at Kensington. She studied, rode, walked, sketched, and played with her various pets. When her fourteenth birthday came, she was—for a few hours—treated like a "grown-up," for at a juvenile ball given in her honor King William led her into the room, and at supper her health was drunk by the whole company.

During the following summer there was more of the educational traveling in which the Duchess believed so firmly and which gave so much pleasure to the people of the country. This summer the Princess and her mother visited chiefly forts, arsenals, lighthouses, and men-of-war. On shipboard they delighted the men by tasting their dinner, and the sailors in return amused them by dancing a hornpipe. Addresses were made; the Princess presented new colors to a regiment; a procession of young girls with flowers and a crown met the royal guests; at one town, whose trade was chiefly in straw, the Princess was presented with a

A QUEEN AT EIGHTEEN

straw bonnet. Wherever she went, her charming grace and cordiality and readiness to be pleased won her lasting friendships.

Throughout the land there was talk about the quiet young girl at Kensington. King William was growing feeble. For half a century England had been ruled by elderly men; how would it fare in the hands of a young girl? Victoria was not as well as she had been, and there were rumors that she would not be equal to the labors of sovereignty. Baroness Lehzen was indignant at the least criticism. "The Princess is not too delicate and she is not too young," declared the lady with her wonted emphasis. "I know all about her, and she will make a greater queen than Elizabeth herself."

An interesting man visited the Princess at this time, Baron Stockmar, who had long been a trusted friend of King Leopold's. "He was the only honest man I ever saw," said a statesman who knew him well, and King William was eager to hear Stockmar's opinion of the young Princess. The Baron had no hesitation in expressing it. "If she were a nobody," he said, "I should say she is gifted with an intelligence beyond her years; but being destined to rule over this great empire, I say that England will grow great and famous under her rule."

"Do you say that?" exclaimed the King. "Then I shall no longer regret that I have no children to hand the crown down to." And yet, some months after this speech was made, the young woman who was to make England great and famous was sent to bed after dancing just one dance at a grand ball given in her honor.

The health of the girl was too precious in the eyes of the Duchess to be wasted in late hours.

Soon after her sixteenth birthday the Princess was confirmed. The ceremony was performed in the chapel of St. James', and none were present except members of the royal family. Even as a child Victoria had often shown great self-control, but when the Archbishop of Canterbury spoke to her, tenderly indeed, but with deep solemnity, of the responsibilities of the life that lay before her, of what good or what harm a single word or deed of hers might cause, then the earnest, conscientious young girl could not remain unmoved. She laid her head on her mother's shoulder and sobbed like a little child.

The wisdom of the watchful mother's care was made manifest in the increasing health and strength of the Princess. She was seen in public far more frequently. The little girl had become a young lady. The plain little white dresses were laid aside, and she now appeared in garments as rich and handsome as were permitted to her youth. One costume that she wore, a pink satin gown and a large pink bonnet, was the special delight of those of her future subjects who had the good fortune to see her in it. This was what she wore when a young American author gazed upon her admiringly and then went away to moralize over the sad fate of royalty. "She will be sold," he said, "bartered away, by those great dealers in royal hearts."

It was true that "dealers in royal hearts" had long before this laid their plans for the disposal of the Princess' affections. King William had proposed five suitors, one after another, but his polite and exasperating sister-in-law had courteously waived all his suggestions. Another scheme had been formed across the water by the Coburg grandmother nearly seventeen years earlier. There was a baby granddaughter in England and a baby grandson in Coburg. If they would only be as fond of each other as the grandmother was of them! Not a word was said to the little English girl, but there is a tradition that when the grandson was but three years old his nurse used to say: "Be a good boy now, Prince Albert, and some day you shall go to England and marry the Queen." However the truth of this story may be, it is certain that not only the grandmother but King Leopold earnestly hoped that some day the Prince might marry the Princess.

When the cousins were seventeen years old, King Leopold thought that the time had come for them to meet; but the wise sovereign had no idea of exposing his warm-hearted little niece to the fascinations of a young man who might not be worthy of her, and he sent the faithful Baron Stockmar to learn all that he could about the character of the Prince. The report was as favorable as the devoted uncle could have wished, and he at once persuaded the Duchess to invite Prince Albert and his brother to spend a month at Kensington.

The two young men arrived and were most royally entertained. Such a round of parties, balls, receptions, dinners, all sorts of festivities, they had never seen. Prince Albert was just a little bored by so much gayety, and acknowledged in his home letters that he had "many hard battles to fight against sleepiness." He seems to have found more pleasure in the quiet hours of walking, sketching, and playing piano duets with the little blue-eyed cousin.

After the brothers had taken their departure, King Leopold wrote his niece, telling her very frankly of his hopes. She replied at once and with equal frankness. One cannot help seeing that the two cousins had become deeply interested in each other, for the letter of the Princess begs her uncle to take special care of one "now so dear to me," and closes with the words, "I hope and trust that all will go on prosperously and well on this subject now of so much importance to me."

There were subjects, however, concerning which all did not go on "prosperously and well." The Princess loved her devoted mother with all her warm heart, and she also loved "Uncle William," who was always good to her. She was now so old that the friction between them could no longer be concealed from her. The King's special grievance was that she was not allowed to visit him save at rare intervals. The "Sailor King" was a favorite among his people, because he was bluff and cheery and witty; but his wit was often coarse, and his good nature not infrequently turned into a "swearing rage" when his humor changed. There were certainly good reasons why the young girl should have been kept from his court; and he was keen enough to see that the Duchess had other grounds than care of her daughter's health for refusing to allow her to visit him. His gentle, stately sister-in-law had outwitted him in every encounter, and at last his wrath burst forth.

A QUEEN AT EIGHTEEN

The time was a state dinner which he gave in honor of his seventy-first birthday. In his speech to the guests he lost all control of himself and declared, "I hope that my life may be spared nine months longer, after which period, in event of my death, no regency will take place. I shall then have the satisfaction of leaving the royal authority to the personal exercise of that young lady"—here the King looked at the Princess Victoria, then, glaring at the Duchess, he roared—"and not in the hands of a person now near to me." He went on like a madman, heaping every kind of abuse upon the Duchess and declaring that she had insulted him by keeping the Princess from his presence.

The Duchess sat like marble, but her daughter burst into tears. At last the dinner came to an end, and the Duchess ordered her carriage that she and the Princess might leave at once instead of spending the night. But Queen Adelaide interposed. "Stay," she said, "stay, I beg of you. The King is ill, he is not himself;" and she whispered, "You have borne so much, bear a little more." The Duchess yielded and remained at the palace until morning.

The nine months passed rapidly, and the morning of May 24, 1837, arrived. The Princess was now eighteen, and the whole land celebrated her coming of age. The day began with a serenade under her window by a band of thirty-seven musicians. One of the songs commenced:

IN THE DAYS OF QUEEN VICTORIA

"Spring renews its golden dreams,
    Sweet birds carol 'neath each spray;
Shed, O sun! thy milder beams
    On the fairest flower of May."

The Princess was delighted with this serenade, but the only song that she asked to have repeated was one that was full of compliments to her mother.

The Union Jack had already been hoisted on the church in Kensington, and its greeting was responded to from the palace by a banner of white silk whereon was "Victoria" in letters of blue. Almost every house had its flag or its bit of decoration of some sort. The King sent a birthday gift of a handsome piano, and that was only the beginning, for all day long costly presents were arriving. Addresses of congratulation were sent by numerous cities and by many public bodies, and the house was thronged with callers. The greatest nobles of the kingdom, the people of most wealth, and the greatest statesmen hastened to Kensington to give their best wishes to the young girl. In the evening a state ball, the most splendid affair of the kind that had been known, was given for her at the Palace of St. James', but the illness of the King kept both him and Queen Adelaide away from the festivities. Between the dances the Princess was escorted to the chair of state. Before this the Duchess had always stood first, but now the young girl who was to rule England took precedence of even her mother.

The way of the Princess to the throne seemed very clear, but there was one man in England who was determined that she should never reach it. He was the Duke of Cumberland, Victoria's uncle. He was the next younger brother of the Duke of Kent, and had it not been for the birth of his niece, the throne of England would have been his own. At that time the sovereign of England was also ruler of Hanover, but Hanover had a law called the Salic law, which forbade any woman to be its monarch. Two or three years earlier the Duke of Cumberland had confided to an English officer his desire to gain the crown.

"The Salic law prevents the Princess Victoria from ruling Hanover," he said, "and therefore she has no right to rule England. If I should be proclaimed king, would you and your troop follow me through London?"

"Yes, and to the Tower the next day!" the officer answered indignantly.

"What will the Princess do for you?" demanded the Duke. "If I were king, I could make you a great man. But this is nothing. I only asked to see what you would say."

The Duke was in earnest, however—so much in earnest that he even ventured to allow his wishes to become known to King William. One day when the two brothers were dining together, the Duke proposed the toast, "The King's health, God save the King!" This was drunk, and then the Duke proposed a second toast, "The King's heir, God bless him!" Both the brothers had drunk too much, but King William was equal to the occasion. He called out, "Drink to the

King's heir, God bless *her!*" and the toast was drunk by all except the Duke.

Nevertheless, the Duke of Cumberland did not give up his wild scheme. He knew that he himself was by no means a favorite in England, and that he had no friends whose devotion would place him upon the throne; but he fancied that he could arouse opposition to the Princess and so open a way for himself to become sovereign. There was nothing to be said against her, but he did his best to arouse dislike to her family. "The Coburgs are the people who have influence with her," he said. "King Leopold has just married a Roman Catholic princess, and the cousin of Victoria has married Queen Maria of Portugal, who is also a Roman Catholic. King William cannot live long, and England will have on its throne not only a child but a child who will be no Protestant."

Now for a century and a half England had had a law that as a Protestant country it must be ruled by a Protestant, and that the husband or wife of the sovereign must also be a Protestant. If Victoria had become a Roman Catholic, she would have forfeited the throne at once. This argument of the Duke of Cumberland was, therefore, almost too absurd to notice; but England was too loyal to the young girl at Kensington not to be in a storm of indignation.

Even then the Duke of Cumberland fancied that he might still have a chance, and he was so insane as to go to that sternly loyal old soldier, the Duke of Wellington, and ask what he thought was the best thing to do.

"To do?" cried the "Iron Duke." "Get out of this country as fast as you can, and take care you don't get pelted as you go."

In less than a month after the eighteenth birthday of the Princess came the night of June nineteenth. The country knew that King William was dying. The Royal Life Guards were at their barracks, but not to sleep. The sentries were doubled. Every horse was saddled, and by it stood its master, ready to race to Windsor to guard the lifeless body of the King, or to gallop to Kensington to escort the girl Queen to her throne.

All that night the officers sat in the messroom and talked of the Princess.

"I saw her on horseback," said one. "She rides superbly, but she looks like a child."

"The Duke of Sussex says the little ones have the brains," remarked another.

"She's a queen, every inch of her," one declared, "and I tell you that England is going to be greater than it ever was before. She's a soldier's daughter, too. King William was a sailor. He could not have held a review to save his—What's that?" The young man broke off abruptly, for the gallop of a horse was heard in the courtyard. There was dead silence in the messroom. In a few minutes the Colonel entered. He held up his hand for attention, but he did not need to do this, for every ear was strained.

"Gentlemen," he said, "King William is dead. Let us drink to the health of the Queen. God save the Queen!"

Early in the morning the Life Guards were ordered to go, part of them to Windsor to do honor to the dead King, part of them to Kensington to do honor to the young Queen.

Meanwhile the Archbishop of Canterbury and Lord Conyngham, the Lord Chamberlain, had been driving at full speed from Windsor to Kensington. Not a person was stirring about the palace, and the only sound heard was the singing of birds. The two men rang, but there was no response. They knocked, they thumped, and they pounded. Finally a very sleepy porter opened the gate and let them into one of the lower rooms of the palace. No one came to them, and at last they rang for a servant.

"Tell the attendant of the Princess Victoria," said the Lord Chamberlain, "that we have come to see her on business of the utmost importance."

The servant withdrew, but no one appeared. They rang again, and at last the attendant of the Princess came to them.

"The Princess Victoria is sleeping," she said, "and she must not be awakened."

Then said the Lord Chamberlain: "We are come on business of state to *the Queen*, and even her sleep must give way to that."

There was no more delay. The Duchess was called, and she awoke her daughter, who still slept in a bed beside her own. "The King is dead," she said. "Lord Conyngham is here, and he wishes to see you. You must not keep him waiting."

The Princess threw on a long white dressing gown and stopped at the door for her mother to accompany her.

"No," said the Duchess. "He wishes to see the Queen alone."

For the first time the young girl was required to stand by herself, and as she stepped over the threshold she left all her free, girlish life behind her. She went down the stairs in her long white dressing gown, with her fair hair falling over her shoulders. As she entered the room, Lord Conyngham knelt before her, kissed her hand, and presented a paper, the formal certificate of the King's death.

Then the Archbishop said: "Your Royal Highness, Queen Adelaide wished me to accompany Lord Conyngham, for she thought that you would be glad to hear how peaceful and quiet the King was at the last."

To the young Queen the sight of the Archbishop brought no thought of the glories of the throne, but rather of those solemn words that he had spoken to her in the chapel of St. James' two years before. With tears in her eyes she said to him, "I beg your Grace to pray for me."

Messengers had been sent to the members of the Privy Council to summon them to immediate attendance at Kensington. When they arrived, they were shown into the ante-chamber in which were the Duke

IN THE DAYS OF QUEEN VICTORIA

of Sussex, uncle of the Queen; the Duke of Wellington, Lord Melbourne, the Prime Minister, and a few others. The doors were closed and an address of loyalty was read aloud and then signed by all present.

In the great saloon adjoining were the Queen and her mother. The Duchess withdrew, and when the doors were opened, there stood near the threshold the slender figure of the girl Queen, looking even slighter and younger than she was in her close-fitting dress of black silk. It was perfectly plain; her hair was parted and drawn back smoothly from her forehead; and she wore not a single ornament. The Duke of Sussex stepped forward to meet her, put his arm around her and kissed her. The others kissed her hand. The address was given to the usher, and the doors between the two rooms were closed. Not a word had been spoken.

A little later in the day came the famous First Council. Lord Melbourne had told the Queen just what was to be done and what her part would be. The Council assembled, and the Lord President read the formal announcement of the death of King William. Then he requested the Prime Minister and several others to go to the Queen and inform her also of the King's death. This was done with as much ceremony as if she had known nothing of it before. When they returned, the proclamation of her accession was read. Then the doors into the adjoining saloon were thrown open, and the Queen stepped forward, wearing a plain, simple mourning dress. Her two uncles, the Duke of Cumberland and the Duke of Sussex, went forward to meet her and led her into the room.

A QUEEN AT EIGHTEEN

At the end of a long table a platform had been placed, and on the platform was the chair of state. The Queen bowed to the Councilors and took her seat in this chair. She read her speech at once, clearly and with as much calmness and dignity as her mother could have shown. It closed, "I shall steadily protect the rights and promote to the utmost of my power the happiness and welfare of all classes of my subjects."

She signed the usual oath insuring the liberty of the Church of Scotland, and then came the solemn swearing of each Councilor to be faithful to her. Her two uncles were sworn first, and as the Duke of Cumberland kissed her hand, she blushed as any other young girl might have done to have an elderly man, her own uncle, kneel at her feet. She kissed him and also the Duke of Sussex. This second uncle was too feeble to make his way to her easily, and she rose from her seat and stepped toward him. After the swearing of the Dukes, the oath was taken by the other members of the Council. When this had been done, she rose and left the room, led by her two uncles.

Never were men more surprised than these experienced Councilors, who thought that they understood all kinds of people and knew what sort of behavior to expect from them.

"I am amazed," said Sir Robert Peel. "She is as modest as a child, but she is firm and self-possessed, and she understands her position perfectly."

Greville, the Clerk of the Council, said: "William IV. came to the throne at sixty-five, and he was so excited that he nearly went mad. The young queen is neither dazzled nor confounded, but she behaves with all the sedateness and dignity the want of which was so conspicuous in her uncle."

The Duke of Wellington was never weary of praising her behavior. "Lord Melbourne was far more nervous than she," said the Duke. "He did not dare to take his eyes off her for fear she might say or do the wrong thing. He need not have been afraid. She is born to rule, and if she had been ten years younger she would have done it equally well; such a bit of a girl as she is," he added; and he finished by saying emphatically, "If she had been my own daughter, I could not have wished that she should do better."

And the good Baroness Lehzen said with tears in her honest blue eyes, "I knew it, I knew my Princess."

There were yet Cabinet Ministers for the Queen to meet, there were matters little and matters great to think of, and the next morning there was to be another Council meeting and the observance of the ancient custom of proclaiming a new sovereign to the public; but the young girl found time in this first day of her dominion to write a letter of sympathy to her "Aunt Adelaide." She addressed it as usual to "Her Majesty the Queen." When she was reminded that the widow of King William was no longer "Queen," but "Queen Dowager," she replied, "I know that her position is altered, but I will not be the first to remind her of the change."

CHAPTER V

THE CORONATION

WHEN the young Queen awoke on the morning after her accession, she must have fancied for a moment that she had dreamed all the events of the previous day. She had gone to bed expecting a quiet morning of study; she had been aroused to hear that she was a queen. Thus far she had remained in her own hone, and had merely received those who had come to her, the Prime Minister, the Councilors, and others; but when she had been Queen for a little more than twenty-four hours, the time had come for her to go to London and be proclaimed sovereign of England in the presence of thousands of her subjects.

Victoria and her mother came out of the palace followed by Lord Melbourne. Both ladies were in mourning. The young Queen wore a black dress with white at the neck and wrists. Her bonnet was black and, in comparison with the great pink one that had so delighted her subjects, it was very small. In front of the royal carriage were the Life Guards, a magnificent body of men, everyone drawing himself up to his full height in his pride that it was *his* company that was to escort the Queen on her first appearance. She bowed to them first, then to the crowds that thronged about the entrance. She and her mother entered the carriage. More of the Life Guards followed and a long line of carriages filled with lords and ladies.

The carriages did not go rapidly, for every road and lane and passage way was full of people, who cheered and waved banners and shouted "God save the Queen!"

When they arrived at St. James', the officers of state stood waiting to receive them, and they were escorted to a window overlooking the quadrangle below, which had long been filled with a great crowd of enthusiastic people.

"Make way for his Grace, the Garter King-at-Arms!" cried the heralds, and that officer advanced, escorted by the Earl-Marshal, gave one look over the assembled people, then waved his scepter for silence, and read the formal proclamation of Victoria as Queen of Great Britain and Ireland. He was glittering in all the insignia of his office, but the eyes of the people were not on him; they were turned toward an upper window, where against a background of crimson curtains stood the slender figure of the Queen, accompanied by her mother and the Prime Minister. The last words of the proclamation were "God save the Queen!" and "God save the Queen!" repeated the bands in a great outburst of martial music. The trumpets sounded, the cannon in the park roared, and the cannon in the Tower roared in response. The people in the court cheered, and the people outside the court

THE CORONATION

cheered. They waved their handkerchiefs, hats, canes, umbrellas, anything that they could wave. They could not be induced to leave the place, and thousands hung about the entrance to the palace for hours, hoping for just one glimpse of their sovereign.

Not long after this proclamation, the Queen presided over another Council meeting, and did it, so said one who was present, "as if she had done nothing else all her life." This was not the end of the day by any means, for now the reception of archbishops, bishops, and judges followed. She met them with the most perfect dignity; but she was a merry young girl as well as a queen, and after she had received the bishops and had withdrawn from the room with a most stately demeanor, they were greatly amused to see her running down the corridor like a child just let out of school. Her Majesty had forgotten that the door was made of glass!

While all this rejoicing was going on, the dead King lay in state at Windsor Palace, shrouded in a crimson pall and under a purple canopy. The crowns of England and of Hanover lay above him. There were banners and imperial escutcheons. Around him were nobles, admirals, and guardsmen. Nearest stood the feeble old Duke of Sussex in his scarlet uniform. The Dead March sounded, and the long line moved slowly on and down to St. George's Chapel. The last honors were duly paid to the dead King, but the thoughts of all the land were with the young Queen.

Before the day had closed, Victoria and her mother were escorted back to Kensington by the Life

Guards to spend a short time before the Queen should take up her abode in Buckingham Palace. "I do not want to go there," she said to the Duke of Sussex. "I love the old Kensington Gardens, where I can wander about as I please. Buckingham Palace is far too big and too grand for me."

Other people may choose their homes, but sovereigns are less free, and there was nothing to do but to leave the homelike Kensington, where her greatest troubles had been an occasional hard lesson, and go to Buckingham, or the New Palace, as it was called, which was to be her London residence.

The New Palace was not yet completed, but men had been working night and day to prepare it for the Queen. It stood on a desolate sand-flat. There were dirty alleys and mud-puddles and dingy little hovels around it, but the coming of the Queen was to make it gorgeous. A splendid new throne, all dazzling in its crimson and gold, was built for her.

"Is it as your Majesty would have it?" inquired the builder.

"It's the most comfortable throne I ever sat on," replied the merry young sovereign.

Buckingham was not lonely by any means. From over the whole country came delegations from universities, corporations, and all kinds of societies. One of these delegations was composed of Quakers, who believe that to uncover the head is to show to man a reverence that should be shown to God alone, and they marched up the stairway without removing their

THE CORONATION

broad-brimmed gray hats. This could not be allowed, but the delegates could hardly be forbidden to see their Queen. Someone was quick-witted enough to discover a way out of the dilemma. "The Quakers won't take off their hats," he whispered, "but it is against their principles to resist violence, and they won't object if we do it for them." Two of the attendants then respectfully raised each man's hat as he passed between them, and returned it to his head when the audience had come to an end.

At the death of a sovereign, Parliament is always dissolved, and a new election is held. Victoria had stood by her "Aunt Adelaide's" side and seen the grand procession which marked the prorogation, but now the time had come for her to take the principal place in the procession.

"It would be better to remain away and allow your speech to be read for you," said both her mother and her physician. "Remember how much you have been through within the past month, and avoid this unnecessary excitement."

The little Queen was wiser than her watchful advisers. She knew well that her subjects had thronged every road leading to Buckingham because they wanted to see her, and she meant to gratify them and appear in all the splendor that a prorogation demanded. As to being exhausted by these ceremonials, she laughed at the idea of such a thing. "I like it all," she said. "I have lived so quietly that it is new to me. It isn't tiresome, it is amusing."

IN THE DAYS OF QUEEN VICTORIA

Therefore "Victoria Regina" was written in letters of gold about a beautiful new throne in the House of Lords. Mr. Davys, her "good, kind master," as she called him, heard her practice her speech; then she was made ready for the ceremony. There were no more simple white muslin dresses for her. She wore a kirtle of white satin and over it a crimson velvet robe with border of ermine. The kirtle flashed with gold embroidery, and the velvet robe was confined by a heavy golden cord and tassels. Diamonds glittered and sparkled in her bracelets and coronet and on her stomacher. A few years before, the young girl had walked to the milliner's and home again, carrying her new bonnet in her hand; but now she seated herself in the royal carriage and was drawn by eight cream-colored horses. The Yeomen of the Guard rode before her; and so she went to the House of Parliament.

The band played "God Save the Queen," as she entered the House of Lords and was conducted to the throne on which "Victoria Regina" was written. It was fortunate that she had no farther to walk, for before she seated herself, the lords-in-waiting laid upon her shoulders the heavy parliamentary mantle of purple velvet.

The brilliant company of peers and bishops remained standing. "My lords, be seated," said the Queen. The usual forms of business were followed, but all interest centered in the speech of the sovereign. Mr. Davys had tutored her well, and when she had finished, Fanny Kemble, the greatest actress of the day, declared, "I never heard any spoken words more musical in their gentle distinctness." Charles Sumner wrote,

THE CORONATION

"I never heard anything better read in my life;" and the Queen's kind old uncle, the Duke of Sussex, could only wipe his eyes and murmur, "Beautiful!"

It was not long before the court moved to Windsor Palace. The ordinary routine of the Queen's day was breakfast with her mother between eight and nine, followed by an hour or two with Lord Melbourne attending to matters of state. Then came an audience with the Cabinet Ministers, whenever there was business to be transacted. About two o'clock the Queen and some twenty or thirty of the ladies and gentlemen of the court took a horseback ride of two hours or longer. After this came music or amusement of some kind until the dinner hour. If there were any children in the palace, the Queen was always ready to spend this time with them, and their company must have been a great relief after the formalities of the day. Dinner was at about half-past seven. After dinner came music, games, dancing, and conversation. This was the order of the day when it was not broken into, but it was almost always broken into, for there were balls, receptions, concerts, banquets, and the reception of delegations.

One visit which was soon paid to the court of England gave the Queen special delight. It was that of her uncle, King Leopold, and his Queen. Victoria had never played the hostess before, but there could have been no one else to whom she would have been so glad to show honor; and now there was a merry time, indeed, for the English Queen planned picnics, dinner parties, sailing parties, and all sorts of gayeties.

Those who looked on from the outside thought of the Queen as a light-hearted young girl enjoying to the full what was almost her first taste of gayety and pleasure, but there was quite another side to her life. More was required of the sovereign of England than to sit on a throne and wear handsome dresses and jewels. There was much hard work for her to do, and this merry little Queen had no thought of attempting to escape it. Those morning hours with Lord Melbourne were hours when she must give her keenest thought and closest attention. At an age when many girls have little more responsibility than to learn a lesson or to choose a dress, this girl had to read complicated papers, to listen to arguments on difficult subjects, and sometimes to decide whether a man proven guilty of crime should live or die. Of course she might have made all this much easier for herself by simply writing her name wherever her Ministers advised, but she would not sign any paper without reading and understanding it.

"Your Majesty," said Lord Melbourne one day, "there is no need of your examining this paper, as it is of no special importance."

"But it is of special importance to me," replied the Queen, "whether I sign a paper with which I am not thoroughly satisfied."

Papers of all sorts were showered upon her. Sometimes after listening to Lord Melbourne's advice she would come to a decision on the first reading, but often she would say, "I must think about this before I sign it." Never was a sovereign so overwhelmed with

THE CORONATION

papers, and her friends began to suspect that some of the officials who wished to have matters go their own way were trying to disgust her with public business, hoping that after a little while she would become so tired of it that she would sign whatever was sent her. They did not know that they were dealing with a Queen who had had to finish her haycocks when she was a little girl. Even Lord Melbourne used to say laughingly, "I'd rather manage ten kings than one queen."

There could hardly have been a better man than Lord Melbourne for the difficult position of adviser to a young woman who was also a queen. He was three times her age, and while his manner to her was always one of most profound respect, he showed an almost fatherly feeling for the fatherless young girl. He was her Prime Minister and was also her trusted friend. Before she became Queen, he had won her confidence in a remarkable way, by opposing her desires and those of her mother. In one of those constantly recurring differences between King and Duchess, he had stood firmly for the King's wishes, because he was the King's servant, although he knew that in a few months at most the Princess would be on the throne. Victoria was wise enough to see that the man who would be faithful even at the probability of his own loss was the man whom she might safely trust, and she did trust him implicitly.

Another member of the Queen's household was the honest Baron Stockmar. He had been sent by King Leopold, as soon as his royal niece had attained her eighteenth birthday, to guard her interests and advise her if it should be necessary. With people in general he was quiet and reserved. At table he "ate nothing and talked less," according to the description of one who was at the court; but all felt that the Queen was especially frank with him, and that he and Lord Melbourne were in perfect agreement. One other duty he had at the English court which was known only to himself and King Leopold, and that was to prepare the way for the marriage that the King hoped would come about between his niece and his nephew. The two young people were really in training for sovereignty. King Leopold kept Prince Albert with him for nearly a year after Victoria's accession. He saw to it that the young man should acquire a good knowledge of English and of the English constitution. Baron Stockmar was in the meantime teaching the Queen the rightful position of the sovereign of England. "The sovereign must belong to no party," he said. "Whatever party is in power has been put in power by the nation, and has a right to claim the loyalty of the Queen."

Of course the devoted Baroness Lehzen had followed her beloved pupil, for one of the first acts of the Queen was to appoint her private secretary. The Baroness said: "I copy all her private correspondence just as I used to do when she was my Princess, and she is as frank with me as when she was a child; but she has never shown me a state document or said a word to me about any state business. She knows that such matters should go to her advisers, and not to me or any other woman."

Surely the little Queen was not without good friends. There were King Leopold, the wisest sover-

THE CORONATION

eign in Europe; Baron Stockmar, the "only honest man"; Lord Melbourne, who seemed to have no thought but for her, and Baroness Lehzen, who had loved her from her babyhood. The position of her mother was very peculiar and not agreeable in all respects. For eighteen years her only aim in life had been to prepare her daughter for the throne of England. The daughter was now on the throne, and the Duchess felt that her occupation was gone. She realized that matters of state must be discussed with the councilors only, and for this she was prepared; but it was not a pleasant surprise to find that the young girl who less than a year before her accession had meekly left the ballroom for bed at her mother's bidding was now manifesting very decided opinions of her own. The Duchess had the fullest confidence in one of the executors of her husband's will, and she would have been glad that he should hold some office in the new government. The Queen treated her mother with the most tender affection, and she willingly granted the gentleman a generous pension, but she refused to have anything to do with him.

Victoria had ascended the throne, but she had never yet worn the English crown, for though a young girl may become a queen in a moment, a coronation is a different matter. "The King is dead, and therefore Victoria is Queen," declared the Council, and she was Queen; but the preparations for a coronation require more time than does the writing of an address of loyalty, and it was a whole year before these preparations were completed. It was not an easy task to decide just what ceremonies should be observed. One matter to

IN THE DAYS OF QUEEN VICTORIA

be seriously deliberated upon was whether the left cheek of the young girl should be forced to endure six hundred kisses of state from the six hundred nobles and bishops. There was not even a crown suited to the occasion, for the old one weighed seven pounds, and the most devoted admirers of the ancient usages could not ask that the "little Queen" should carry that load on her head. After many lengthy consultations, these momentous questions were decided. The tradesmen were assured that there would be enough ceremony to bring about large sales, the peers and bishops were told that they would not be allowed to kiss the pink cheek of the Queen, and the crown jewelers were bidden to set to work on a new crown that should weigh only half as much as the old one.

The day came at last, June 28, 1838. London evidently meant to make the most of it, and as soon as the eager watchers saw the first glimpse of dawn, a salute of twenty-one cannon was fired. It was only a little after three o'clock, but the earliness of the hour made little difference to the thousands that had been up all night. Some had stayed up to be sure of securing a good place to see the procession, some because the services of the hairdressers were in such demand that, when a head was once in order, no risk of disarrangement could be ventured upon, and some had been kept awake by pure excitement and nervousness. There was no sleeping after daylight for anyone, for those who were far enough from the Tower to drowse through the firing of cannon were aroused by the ringing of bells which followed, as every church tower rang out its merriest chimes. At five o'clock Westminster

THE CORONATION

Abbey was opened, and this was none too early, for the people who were fortunate enough and rich enough to obtain tickets had long been thronging the entrance. These people in the Abbey had a long time to wait, for it was fully ten o'clock before the salute of twenty-one guns from the park gave the signal that the procession had started from Buckingham Palace.

Such a procession as it was! First came the trumpeters, then the Life Guards, bands, foreign ambassadors in most gorgeous carriages, more Life Guards, the carriage of the Duchess of Kent, the Duke of Sussex, and others of the royal family, the officers of the royal household, and the Yeomen of the Guard. Then all the thousands along the way were agape, for the eight cream-colored horses were seen drawing the chariot of state, wherein sat the pretty little maiden who was the center and cause of all this magnificence. A circlet of diamonds was on her head. She wore a dress of gold tissue, and a mantle of crimson velvet trimmed with gold lace and lined with ermine. Pearls and diamonds gleamed and flashed at every motion. With her rode the Mistress of the Robes and the Master of the Horse. A body of cavalry followed her.

The procession was nearly an hour and a half in reaching the Abbey, for the Queen would not go by the shortest way. All that time people were shouting, and banners were waving, for every house along the line of march was brilliant with as much decoration as its owner could afford. Half a million strangers were in London, and many houses were rented at enormous rates. Five or six thousand dollars was not looked upon as a rental at all exorbitant, and some were let at a much higher price.

At the door of the Abbey, the Queen was met by the chief officers of state. She walked slowly up the aisle, but not alone by any means. Heralds, clergy, and officers of state came first; then a noble bearing the coronet of the Duchess of Cambridge, followed by the Duchess herself, with her long train of purple velvet. Another coronet was borne on a silken cushion, and after it came the Duchess of Kent. Then came six nobles, each carrying some piece of the regalia. There were dukes and earls and marquises and generals and field marshals and bishops, all in their most brilliant array. A little whisper, "The Queen, the Queen!" ran through the long lines of peers and peeresses and ambassadors and judges. It was followed by the waving of handkerchiefs and scarfs and such shouts of applause as shook the Abbey to its foundations, and Victoria advanced, escorted by three bishops. Eight young girls in white silk and silver, with blush roses, carried her train. Then came members of the royal household, gentlemen-at-arms, lords-in-waiting, and other officials without number.

All this time the choir were singing "I was glad when they said unto me, Let us go into the house of the Lord." Then they sang "God save the Queen!" and the trumpets sounded the accompaniment. A most impressive moment followed. The trumpets ceased, every voice was hushed, not a sound was heard among all the thousands in the vast Abbey. The Queen had passed through the door looking "like a young girl on her birthday," but now her face was grave, and she

THE CORONATION

knelt before the altar for a moment of silent prayer. By an ancient privilege, the Westminster schoolboys had the right to give the first greeting to the sovereign, and as she rose, the Abbey rang with their shouts, "Victoria! Victoria! Vivat Victoria Regina!"

The next part of the ceremony is known as the "Recognition"—that is, the recognition of the new sovereign as the lawful sovereign. The Queen and the Archbishop of Canterbury turned to the north, and the Archbishop said: "Sirs, I here present unto you Queen Victoria, the undoubted Queen of this realm; wherefore, all you who are come this day to do your homage, are you willing to do the same?" "God save Queen Victoria!" the people cried. The Archbishop and the Queen then turned to the south, to the east, and to the west, and the same words were repeated with the same response. This signified that the people of the land had formally accepted her as their sovereign.

After this, the Queen, followed by the eight train-bearers, walked to the altar, and she made an offering of a golden altar cloth and a pound's weight of gold. This was only the beginning of the four-hours' ceremony, and next came a long sermon preached by the Bishop of London, followed by the solemn oath of the Queen to be just and govern according to the law.

Then came the act of coronation, but for this Victoria was not to appear in jewels and ermine. She was escorted to one of the chapels and robed in a flowing gown of fine white muslin. Over this was thrown a robe of gold brocade worked with the rose, the shamrock, and the thistle, emblematic of England,

IN THE DAYS OF QUEEN VICTORIA

The Coronation of Queen Victoria,
in Westminster Abbey, June 28th, 1838

Ireland, and Scotland. In this quaint and ancient costume she knelt before the altar. The Archbishop led her to the famous old chair of St. Edward, wherein was the stone of Scone, and touched her head and hands with the holy oil. The scepter, orb, sword, and other things signifying power and authority in either Church or state, were handed to her, each with a few words from the Archbishop, exhorting her to use it properly. The ruby ring was placed upon her finger, and the cloth-of-gold mantle upon her shoulders. Then the Archbishop slowly lifted the crown, which was blazing with diamonds, sapphires, rubies, and emeralds, and placed it upon her head. The next moment all the peers and peeresses lifted their coronets and put them on. The whole building flashed and glittered until one might have fancied that it was raining diamonds. "God save the Queen!" echoed and re-echoed. The thousands who stood outside the Abbey caught up the cry, the bells of all the churches in London began to ring, and the guns of all the garrison towns were fired.

The ceremony of homage followed. The Archbishop, the two royal dukes, and many other dukes, marquises, earls, viscounts, and barons knelt and, kissing her hand, said: "I do become your liege man of life and limb, and of earthly worship, and faith and truth I will bear unto you, to live and die against all manner of folk, so help me God!" One of the peers was so aged and infirm that he tried twice in vain to ascend the steps. The Queen rose and moved toward him and extended her hand to him as simply and naturally as any other young girl might have done who was not sitting on a throne. After the homage, she received the Holy Sacrament; the "Hallelujah Chorus" was sung; and then the procession re-formed and went slowly over the way to Buckingham Palace.

When George III. was crowned, he complained of some blunders that were made, but he could hardly have been much comforted by the reply that matters would "go better next time." Even though Victoria was the third sovereign crowned since the time of George III., there were still some mistakes. England was accustomed to crowning strong men, but not slender young girls, and the orb was made so heavy that holding it was very wearisome, while the ruby ring was made for the little finger and had to be forced upon the ring finger as best it could be. When the peers did homage, they were required to touch the crown; and the Queen said it was fortunate that she had had it made as tight as possible, for many of them knocked it, and one actually clutched it.

After such a day as this, Victoria must have felt that she was "really and truly" a queen; but with all her dignity and her royalty, she was still a frank, natural young girl, and the story is told that when she entered Buckingham Palace and heard the bark of her favorite dog, she exclaimed, "Oh, there's Dash! I must go and give him his bath."

The English were proud of their Queen, of her dignity and her royal bearing, but it was these touches of frankness and simplicity that won their hearts, and made them feel that with all her jewels, her velvets, and her ermine, she was, after all, one of themselves. It was at this time that the Duke of Sussex wrote to a

THE CORONATION

friend: "The girl Queen is becoming more and more popular. You would simply idolize her if you saw that bright little face, with clear blue eyes, winning all hearts and making us all say, 'God save the Queen!'"

CHAPTER VI

THE COMING OF THE PRINCE

THE coronation ceremonies in Westminster Abbey were, indeed, magnificent, but it must not be supposed that England was satisfied with no further celebration of so joyful an event. Throughout the realm there were for several days fairs, balls, and entertainments of all kinds. London was illuminated, and the theaters were made free to all who chose to attend them. People's hearts and purses were opened. The rich were not satisfied with having a good time themselves; they wanted the children of the land and the poor to have a good time also. In many places feasts were given, and one of the most famous of these was held in a great open field in Cambridge, where more than fourteen thousand persons were entertained.

In the center of the field was a space for the band, and around it a platform. Much money had been subscribed for the feast, but the committee felt sure that large numbers of people would be ready to pay from seventy-five cents to one dollar and a half for the privilege of walking about on this platform and seeing what was to be seen. They were right, for there was "a most fashionable and select company," who promenaded around the circular platform and watched the feasters.

Sixty tables, each two hundred and thirty feet long, stretched out from the central platform like the rays of a star; and when the signal was given, the fourteen thousand persons, poor people and children of all ages, marched to their places. It must have been an amusing procession, for each one was obliged to bring his own plate, knife, fork, and mug for beer. There was roast beef, and there were various other good things; but the member of the committee who wrote the account of the dinner seems to have been especially interested in the puddings. "Beautiful puddings," he says they were, and he tells just where each one was boiled. He states, too, that 2475 pounds of raisins were put into them.

At the end of the dinner, pipes, tobacco, and snuff were passed to the grown folk. There was a salute of nineteen guns in honor of the Queen's nineteen years. A balloon, which the enthusiastic committeeman calls a "stupendous machine," was sent up, and the health of the Queen was drunk. The Sunday-school children sang a song of better intention than rhyme, which began:

> "Victoria! Victoria!
>   We hail thy gentle rule;
> Victoria! the Patroness
>   Of every Sunday school."

After the singing, came various games and contests. Men tried to climb a well-soaped pole to get a leg of mutton which was fastened to the top. Others were tied into sacks and jumped as far as possible in the attempt to win a pair of boots. There was a wheelbarrow race run by ten blindfolded men. A pig was offered to the man who could catch the animal and swing it over his shoulder by the well-greased tail. Men grinned through horse-collars to see who could make the ugliest face and so win a pair of new trousers. Six boys with their hands tied behind their backs were given penny loaves and molasses, and a new hat was waiting for the one who ate his loaf first. Other boys with their hands tied were "bobbing for apples"—that is, trying to lift apples with their teeth from a tub of water—and another group of boys were struggling to see who could first swallow a penny-worth of dry biscuit, and so win a new waistcoat. There were foot races and donkey races and hurdle races, and races among men each with one leg tied up. At last the day came to an end with fireworks, and all the happy, tired people went home, fully convinced that under this new sovereign their country would be more prosperous than ever.

It seems very strange that this Queen who was worshiped by her people in the summer of 1838 should in the course of a few months have become exceedingly unpopular with some of her subjects, but so it was. There were in England two political parties, the Whigs and the Tories. Queen Victoria's sympathies were with the Whigs. They were in power when she came to the throne, but in the spring of 1839 the

THE COMING OF THE PRINCE

Cabinet proposed an important bill which Parliament refused to make a law. Under such circumstances it is the custom for the Prime Minister and the Cabinet to resign, because such a refusal is supposed to signify that the people, whom Parliament represents, do not approve of their acts.

When Lord Melbourne told the Queen that he must resign, she felt very badly. She must stand at the head of a great nation, and the one in whose advice she had trusted could advise her no longer. The leaders of the Tories were "the Duke," as the Duke of Wellington was called, and Sir Robert Peel; and Lord Melbourne told her that her wisest course would be to ask the Duke to become her Prime Minister and select a Cabinet of Tories. The Duke had declared before this that he did not know what the Tories would do for a Prime Minister if they should come into power. "I have no small talk," he said, "and Peel has no manners;" but when the Queen sent for him, of course he obeyed. She asked him to be her Prime Minister, and said to him honestly: "I cannot help being very sorry to make a change and give up my Ministers, especially Lord Melbourne, for he has been almost a father to me."

The straightforward old soldier was delighted with her frankness, but he said: "I am somewhat deaf, and I am too old a man to undertake this work and serve you properly. Moreover, it would be much better for one who can lead the House of Commons to be your Majesty's Prime Minister. I advise you to send for Sir Robert Peel."

IN THE DAYS OF QUEEN VICTORIA

Now, this girl of nineteen did not like the man who had "no manners," but she was a lady as well as a Queen, and when Sir Robert appeared—in full dress, as was required—she received him so courteously that he went away much pleased, having promised to obey her command and form a Cabinet. This was easily done, and the next morning he brought her a list of names.

"But you must not expect me to give up the society of Lord Melbourne," she said.

"Certainly not," was Peel's reply. "Moreover, Lord Melbourne is too honorable a man to attempt to influence your Majesty in any way against the existing government." Sir Robert then suggested several men whom he knew that she liked for various positions of honor in the royal household. Finally he said, perhaps a little bluntly, "It will be desirable to make some changes in the ladies of your Majesty's household." Then a storm arose.

"I shall not part with any of my ladies," declared the Queen.

"But, your Majesty," said Sir Robert, "most of these ladies are closely related to the former Cabinet Ministers." The Queen would not yield, but she was willing to discuss the subject later with him and the Duke. When they appeared before her, they said: "Your Majesty, the ladies of the household are on the same footing as the lords."

"No," declared the Queen, "I have lords besides, and I have let you do with them as you chose. If you had just been put out of office and Lord Melbourne had come in, I am sure that he would not have asked me to give up my ladies."

"There are more Whigs than Tories in the House of Commons," said Peel, "and if these ladies who are closely related to prominent Whigs are retained, all Europe will look upon England as the country that is governed by a party which the sovereign dislikes and in which she has no confidence."

"I give you my lords," replied the Queen steadfastly, "but I keep my ladies." The two nobles were in a dilemma. According to the British constitution, "The Queen can do no wrong"—that is, not she, but the Prime Minister is held responsible for every public act. Sir Robert could not remain Prime Minister if the Queen positively refused to yield to a course which he thought necessary.

While the Tory leaders were trying to plan some way out of the difficulty, the Queen sent a letter to Lord Melbourne which was written in much the same way that an indignant young girl would write to her father. "Do not fear," she said, "that I was not calm and composed. They wanted to deprive me of my ladies, and I suppose they would deprive me next of my dressers and housemaids; they wished to treat me like a girl, but I will show them that I am Queen of England."

Lord Melbourne called his Cabinet together in such haste that one member had to be brought from the opera and another from a dinner party. He read them the Queen's letter, and asked, "What shall we advise?"

"Advise her to give up two or three of her principal ladies," suggested one, "and perhaps that will satisfy Peel."

"Does anyone know exactly what Peel wants," queried another, "and how many ladies he demands shall be removed?" This was an exceedingly sensible question, and if it had been taken to Peel for an answer, the trouble might have been brought to an end. He would probably have been satisfied with the resignation of two or three of the strongest partisans and principal talkers among the ladies; and, although the Queen was insisting upon what she believed was her right, yet much of her indignation arose from her belief that Peel meant to deprive her of all who were then her attendants, perhaps even the Baroness Lehzen. The question was not taken to Peel, however, and the discussion in the Cabinet went on.

"Let us write a letter for the Queen to copy and send to Peel," was the next suggestion, "saying that she will not consent to a course which she believes to be contrary to custom and which is repugnant to her feelings." This suggestion was adopted. The letter was written, and the Queen copied it to send; but before it reached Sir Robert, he resigned his position, and Lord Melbourne was again Prime Minister.

This was the famous "Bedchamber Plot," and it aroused all England. Lord Melbourne and the Whigs said:

THE COMING OF THE PRINCE

"It is a small matter that the Queen should be allowed to retain her favorite attendants."

Sir Robert and the Tories replied:

"The Prime Minister is responsible for the acts of the Queen, and it is a large matter if she refuses to follow his advice when he believes that the good of the realm demands a certain course. She is not the Queen of the whole country, she is only the Queen of the Whigs, and the whole thing is a plot to keep the Whigs in power."

"*We* are loyal to our sovereign," declared the Whigs.

"*We* stand by the constitution of Great Britain, not by the whims of a girl of nineteen," retorted the Tories. The amusing part of the struggle was that the Whigs had always prided themselves on standing by the constitution and the rights of the people, while the Tories had favored increasing the power of the sovereign; but in those days the question was too serious to strike anyone as amusing.

As the weeks of the summer and the early autumn passed, matters only grew worse. Victoria was spoken of most contemptuously, and was even hissed in a public assembly. Mr. Greville wrote in his journal: "The Tories seem not to care one straw for the crown, its dignity or its authority, because the head on which it is placed does not nod with benignity to them." Peel was, of course, above such behavior as that of some of his violent partisans, but he must have been somewhat surprised at developments. He had been afraid that the Queen's opinions and judgment were so weak that she would be influenced by the talk of a few ladies in attendance, and would be unable to judge questions fairly and without prejudice; but he had found that, whatever might be the faults of the young lady on the throne, she could never be accused of having no will of her own.

During the first two years of her reign, the friends of the Queen were watching her with much anxiety. She was an unusual girl, with an unusual training, but, after all, she was only a girl, and she had responsibilities to meet from which, as Carlyle said, "an archangel might have shrunk." Her position was all the more dangerous because she was too young to realize her difficulties; and when trouble arose, there was no one in the land of whom she could ask counsel without arousing the enmity of someone else. Everyone who was capable of advising her was prominent in one political party or the other. If she had discussed any of her hard questions with even her own mother, and it had become evident that suggestions had come from the Duchess of Kent, there would have been talk at once of "foreign influence."

Meanwhile, "foreign influence" in the person of the wise King Leopold was busily at work. The young Queen had reigned for more than two years, and the first novelty of her position had passed. At first it had been delightful to her to feel that she was "the Queen," and that she could do precisely as she chose. Even the Bedchamber Plot had resulted in her having her own way, in keeping her ladies and the Whig Cabinet; but so clear-minded a woman as Queen Victoria must have seen—as, indeed, she declared some years

THE COMING OF THE PRINCE

later—that she had not behaved like a constitutional monarch, and she knew that thousands of her subjects were indignant with her.

Never was a loving uncle more shrewd in his affection than this "wisest sovereign in Europe;" for just at this time, when his niece was feeling far less self-sufficient than she had felt some months earlier, he proposed that Prince Albert and his brother Ernest should pay her a visit. The young men came, bringing with them a letter from the King which spoke of them in most matter-of-fact terms as "good, honest creatures, really sensible and trustworthy." The point of the letter was in its closing sentence, "I am sure that if you have anything to recommend to them, they will be most happy to hear it from you."

The Queen knew very well what this sentence signified, and she was more ready to "recommend" than she would have been some months before. She had seen her cousins only once, and that was more than three years earlier. Prince Albert was then a lovable boy, and the Princess was willing that her relatives should understand that she would marry him some day. When nearly two years had passed and she had become Queen, she felt much older and more mature; but she thought of her cousin as still a boy. She expected to marry him some time in the future, but she was not willing to permit even any formal engagement at that time. King Leopold wrote urging her to make some "decisive arrangement" for the following year. The Queen replied: "Albert and I are both too young to think of marriage at present. He does not know

English well enough, and there are other studies which he needs to pursue."

King Leopold saw that it was of no use to press the question further at that time, and he told the Prince that the marriage would have to be postponed for a few years. The Prince saw the truth in Victoria's objections. He knew that his position in England would demand all the skill and knowledge that he could acquire, and he admitted that her arguments were strong.

"You understand, and you will wait?" asked his uncle.

"Yes," answered the Prince, "I will wait, if I have only some certain assurance to go on; but I do not want to be left in the ridiculous position of Queen Elizabeth's suitors. I do not want all Europe talking for years about my marriage, and then laughing at the announcement that Victoria never meant to marry me."

Another year passed. Then came the Bedchamber trouble. King Leopold watched every item of news from England. "Now is the time," said the sagacious King to himself, and he proposed the visit.

There had been little correspondence between the cousins. Prince Albert had sent the Princess sketches of the places that he had visited in his travels, and when she became Queen, he wrote her a somewhat formal little letter, reminding her that the happiness of millions lay in her hands, and closing rather primly, "I will not be indiscreet and abuse your time."

THE COMING OF THE PRINCE

Victoria must have had in her mind a picture of her cousin that was a strange combination of a serious young man somewhat given to sermonizing, and the stout, merry boy of seventeen who had slipped down to the floor of his carriage and pushed his dog's head up to the window when people pressed around to see the Prince.

With these two conflicting notions in her thoughts, the Queen went to the head of the staircase in Windsor Palace to welcome her "two dear cousins." The stout boy had vanished, but in his place stood a tall, manly, handsome young man, with a cheery, thoughtful face. Two days later a letter went from the Queen to "Uncle Leopold," which said, "My dear Uncle, Albert is fascinating." Then she remembered that she had two cousinly guests and added, "The young men are very amiable, delightful companions, and I am very glad to have them here."

King Leopold wrote at once, "I am sure you will like the cousins the more, the longer you see them." Then he talked about the Prince. "Albert is full of talent and fun and draws cleverly. May he be able to strew roses without thorns on the pathway of life of our good Victoria! He is well qualified to do so."

While the hopeful uncle was writing this letter, Victoria was talking with Lord Melbourne.

"My lord," she said, "I have made up my mind at last, and I am ready to marry Prince Albert whenever he wants me."

"I am very glad of it," replied her fatherly friend. "You will be much more comfortable; for a woman cannot stand alone for any time, in whatever position she may be."

"Do you think that my people will be pleased?" she asked.

"I believe that they will," he replied, for he knew very well how eager they were for her marriage. No one liked the Duke of Cumberland, who was now King Ernest of Hanover, but if the Queen died without children, he would come over to England and wear the English crown as well as that of Hanover. The feeling against him was so strong that it had even been proposed in Parliament to make a law forbidding him ever to occupy the throne.

On the fourth morning of their visit, the two Princes went hunting. It was a long forenoon to the Queen, for she had what she afterwards called a "nervous" thing to do. They came back at noon, but they had hardly time to change their hunting clothes before a message was brought to Prince Albert that the Queen wished to see him.

Now, royal etiquette forbade that this Prince of a little German duchy should ask the sovereign of Great Britain for her hand; so when Albert reached the Queen's apartments, he was obliged to wait until she had spoken.

"I think you must know why I wished you to come," she said shyly. The Prince had still to keep silent; he could only bow, but his bow must have expressed a great deal, for she went on bravely: "It will make me very happy if you will consent to what I wish."

In just what form the Prince made his reply the Queen did not reveal, but it was evidently satisfactory, for she wrote, "He is perfection in every way." That very day she sent a letter to King Leopold in which she said: "I am so much bewildered by it all that I hardly know how to write. But I do feel very happy."

A few weeks before this time she had written Baron Stockmar that she could not think of marrying for three or four years, but that very day she wrote him: "I *do* feel so guilty, I know not how to begin my letter, but I think the news it will contain will be sufficient to insure your forgiveness. Albert has completely won my heart, and all was settled between us this morning. I feel certain that he will make me very happy. I wish I could say," continued the modest little sovereign of Great Britain, "that I felt as certain of making him happy, but I shall do my best."

Prince Albert, too, had some letters to write; and as Victoria had written to King Leopold, his first was to Baron Stockmar. After telling of his happiness and of his love for the Queen, he wrote: "I cannot write more, I am too much bewildered." It certainly was bewildering. He had been told not long before that the Queen was determined not to marry for three or four years at any rate, and that she would not consent to any formal engagement. He had come to England with a determination to insist either that she should recognize the informal engagement between them or that it should be broken off.

The Duchess of Kent had loved Albert from the first, and she was very happy in the thought of the marriage. She and the Baroness Lehzen, together with Lord Melbourne and Prince Albert's brother, were the only ones in England who knew the secret until five or six weeks had passed. Then came a difficult five minutes for the young Queen. She had to meet her Council of eighty middle-aged men and tell them of her engagement. It is no wonder that she "hardly knew who was there." The picture of the Prince in her bracelet gave her courage, and though Lord Melbourne was far down the room, she caught a kind look from him and saw the tears of sympathy in his eyes. Her fingers trembled, but she soon controlled herself and read: "It is my intention to ally myself in marriage with the Prince Albert of Saxe-Coburg and Gotha." She went through the rest of the paper with her usual clear, sweet voice, and one of the Councilors wrote of the event: "Certainly she did look as interesting and as handsome as any young lady I ever saw."

When the reading of the paper was finished, the Lord President asked: "Have we your Majesty's permission to publish this declaration?" The Queen bowed and left the Council Chamber. About two months later she had something even harder to do; she had to open Parliament and ask that an income should be granted to the Prince. Another matter also had to be settled, and that was what position he should hold in England. Whether he should enter a room before or after dukes, earls, and members of the royal family was a question that gave rise to much discussion.

THE COMING OF THE PRINCE

These two questions were not settled as the Queen wished, for the sum granted to the Prince was but three-fifths of what her Ministers had asked, and Parliament refused to pass a law giving him precedence next to herself. The Duke of Wellington said, "Let the Queen put the Prince just where she wishes him to be;" and this she did, as far as England was concerned, by issuing an order in Council that he should stand next to herself. Some of her royal relatives were indignant, and King Ernest declared positively that he would never give precedence to the younger brother of a German duke. "I won't give way to any paper royal highness," he declared. The Queen was both hurt and angry at these decisions; but Prince Albert's only fear was lest they indicated objection to the marriage on the part of the English, and he wrote: "While I possess your love, they cannot make me unhappy."

A little more than a week after this letter was written, the day of the wedding came. It had been the custom to celebrate royal weddings in the evening, though other weddings must by law take place before noon; but on this, as on most other subjects, the Queen had a very definite opinion. "I wish to be married as my subjects are married," she said, "and the ceremony must be at noon."

"Is it the will of your Majesty that the word 'obey' be omitted from the promise that you make to the Prince?" asked the Archbishop of Canterbury.

"No," she answered with decision. "I am not to be married as a queen, but as a woman."

IN THE DAYS OF QUEEN VICTORIA

The Prince Consort

THE COMING OF THE PRINCE

The wedding day was stormy, but that made little difference to bride, groom, or any of the brilliant company assembled in the Chapel of St. James'. The Prince wore the uniform of a British field-marshal, with the collar of the Garter, and looked exceedingly handsome. As he came into the Chapel, the organ burst out into the strains of "See, the Conquering Hero Comes." He stood by the altar waiting for his bride, and in a short time she appeared, escorted by the Lord Chamberlain. She wore a dress of heavy white satin, woven in England. Her veil had made scores of poor women happy, for she had ordered it of the lace-makers of Honiton in Devon. She wore no crown, but only a wreath of orange blossoms. She had diamond earrings and necklace, and a few diamonds in her hair. Twelve bridesmaids in white tulle and white roses bore her train; and a hard time they had, for although it was six yards long, they found it too short for so many bearers. One of them wrote: "We were all huddled together, and scrambled rather than walked along, kicking each other's heels and treading on each other's gowns."

At the moment the ring was placed on the Queen's finger, the guns in the Park and at the Tower were fired, and the bells rang out their merriest peals. When the ceremony was over, the party returned to Buckingham Palace for a wedding breakfast. The bridesmaid who wrote the account of the wedding said that Prince Albert "seemed a little nervous about getting into the carriage with a lady with a tail six yards long," but they all reached the palace in safety. After the breakfast the sunshine at last beamed down upon them, and the young couple sped away for their honeymoon at Windsor Castle.

CHAPTER VII

HOUSEKEEPING IN A PALACE

COMMON people may make a wedding tour, but kings and queens are too fully occupied to afford such luxuries. The sovereign of England could spend her honeymoon in Windsor Castle, but it must be a honeymoon of only four days. Those four days, however, were marked by a freedom which she had never enjoyed before. For the first time in her life she could talk with someone of her own age without having to be on her guard lest what she said should be repeated and do harm.

One of the subjects that needed to be discussed and to be reformed was the royal housekeeping. Many a woman living in a two-room cottage is quite as comfortable as the Queen of Great Britain was in 1840. Three men, the Lord Steward, the Lord Chamberlain, and the Master of the Horse, were supposed to have the management of the household. These persons were men of high rank, and their offices were given them in reward for their political services rather than for their ability to manage the domestic affairs of a palace. Of course they were entirely too stately to take any charge themselves of the housekeeping, and they did not delegate their power to anyone in the palace. Some of the servants were under one of these three, and some were under another. No one was at the head of the house, and everyone did about as he chose. If the Queen rang a bell for a servant, the servant might answer it, or he might be absent from the palace, just as it happened, and the Queen was helpless, for the only one at all responsible was some aristocratic nobleman who was, perhaps, far away on a yachting trip. When the Prime Minister of France was a guest at Windsor, he wandered over the palace for an hour trying to find his bedroom, for there was no one on duty to point it out to him. At last he was sure that he had it, and he opened the door. Behold! there stood a maid brushing the hair of a lady who sat at a toilet table, and could see in the glass the embarrassed gentleman as he hurriedly retreated. The next day he discovered that the lady before the glass was her Majesty. Baron Stockmar wrote that cleaning the inside of the windows belonged to one department and cleaning the outside to another. It is quite probable that when the little Princess Victoria asked Queen Adelaide to let her clean the windows, there was visible need of such work. The servants of one department brought the wood and laid the fire, but it was not their work to light it, and for that duty a servant from another department must be called. A pane of glass could not be mended without the signatures of five different officials. No one was responsible for the cleanness of the house or even for its safety; and if the man whose business it was to guard an entrance preferred to do something else, there was no one to interfere with his pleasure. The doors were indeed so carelessly guarded that one night a boy was found under a sofa in the room next to the Queen's bedroom. He could not be punished as a thief, for he had stolen nothing. He was not a housebreaker, for he had simply walked in through open doors, and no one had been on guard to prevent such intrusions. It was finally decided that he was a vagabond, and he was imprisoned for three months.

Prince Albert was very anxious to have better management of the household, and he laid the matter before the Prime Minister.

"But men of high rank are now eager to hold these offices in the royal household," was the reply, "and it will make trouble if anyone is put over them, or if there is any interference with their departments."

"True," replied the Prince, "but the household machinery is so clumsy and works so ill that, as long as its wheels are not mended, there can be neither order nor regularity, comfort, security, nor outward dignity in the Queen's palace." Reforms began, but the Prince had to work very slowly, and some years passed before either the Queen or her guests could live in comfort.

If the Queen had insisted upon these changes being made at once, many of them could probably have been carried out; but the Bedchamber Plot had taught her that the sovereign must not act contrary to the wishes of her people. There was especial need of care at the time. Within hardly more than half a century, the American colonies had freed themselves from England and become a republic; France had had a terrible revolution; throughout Europe people were thinking of change, of more power for the people and less for the government. In England there was little probability of a revolution, but it was more than two hundred years since there had been any general and lasting enthusiasm for the monarch of the realm; and both Prince Albert and the Queen felt that the only way to make the throne strong and enduring was to win the affection of the people. This was the teaching of Baron Stockmar, the faithful friend and adviser of the royal couple. They appreciated his devotion, and all the more because they could do nothing for him. He did not care for money or office, and he was absolutely independent. When dinner was over, he did not trouble himself to go to the drawing room unless he felt inclined. He would generally spend the winter with the Queen, but he disliked good-bys, and when he wanted to go home to his family, he left the palace without a word of farewell.

Baron Stockmar had good pupils. Prince Albert was not yet twenty-one at the time of his marriage, and the question had arisen whether, as he was not of age, he could legally take the oath that was required of every member of the Council. Soon after the marriage, King Leopold asked an English lady about him.

"Do the English like him? Will he be popular?" inquired the King.

"They call him very handsome," was her reply, "but the English are always ready to find fault with foreigners, and they say he is stiff and German."

HOUSEKEEPING IN A PALACE

As the months passed, however, the English learned that this young Prince was a remarkable man in his grasp of politics, his talent for art and music, and his honest and unselfish devotion to the good of the realm. What was more, they showed their appreciation by an act of Parliament. The country was not yet at rest about the succession to the crown. If the Queen should have a child and die before the child was of age, a regent would be necessary. Parliament discussed the question, and named the Prince, "the foreigner," as regent. "They would not have done it for him six months ago," declared Lord Melbourne with delight.

The Queen had always been loved by the Whigs, and just about this time, a great wave of devotion to her swept through not only their ranks but also those of the Tories. A boy of seventeen tried to shoot her, not because he hated her, but because he wished to be notorious. The Queen was in her carriage with the Prince when the attempt was made. She drove on rapidly to tell the Duchess of Kent that she was safe, then she returned to the park, where hundreds of people had gathered, hoping to see her and make sure that she was not injured. She was received with cheers and shouts of delight, and all the horseback riders formed in line on both sides of her carriage as if they were her bodyguard. When she appeared at the opera a few days later, she was greeted with a whirlwind of cheers and shouts. The whole house sang "God Save the Queen!" Then they pleased her still more by crying, "The Prince! The Prince!" and when Prince Albert stepped to the front, he was cheered so heartily that she knew he was fast winning the hearts of her people.

Operas and popularity were not the only things to be thought of in those days. The royal couple, barely twenty-one years of age, were working hard on constitutional history. They were very anxious, too, about the possibility of war with France on account of trouble in regard to Turkey and Egypt, and when their little daughter was born, in November, 1840, the Queen said: "I really think she ought to be named Turko-Egypto."

The little girl was not named Turko-Egypto, but Victoria Adelaide Mary Louise, and she had to wait three months for her name, as the christening did not take place until February. She was baptized with water brought from the River Jordan. The font was not taken from the Tower, as it had been for her mother's baptism, but a new one was made of silver, marked with her coat-of-arms and also those of her father and her mother. She was a very decorous little Princess, and the proud father wrote home to Coburg that she "behaved with great propriety and did not cry at all."

There was much rejoicing at the birth of this Princess Royal; but when, a year later, a Prince was born, then the delight of the nation knew no bounds. He was the heir to the throne, and it was impossible to do too much to celebrate his birth. *Punch* said:

> "Huzza! we've a little Prince at last,
> A roaring Royal boy;
> And all day long the booming bells
> Have rung their peals of joy.

HOUSEKEEPING IN A PALACE

"And the little Park guns have blazed away
And made a tremendous noise,
Whilst the air has been filled since eleven o'clock
With the shouts of little boys."

One or two questions in regard to the celebration had to be settled by the courts of justice. It was an old privilege that when an heir to the throne was born, the officer on guard at St. James' Palace should be promoted to the rank of major. In this case the child was born at Buckingham, but the guard at St. James' demanded his promotion nevertheless. The matter was complicated by the fact that the change of sentry had chanced to occur just at the time of the birth of the Prince, and whether the old or the new guard actually held the keys was a difficult question to determine. Another difficulty of the same kind arose at Chester. The Prince had the title of Earl of Chester, and the mayor of that city declared that by ancient right he had claim to a baronetcy. Exactly the same question arose as with the sentinels, for at about the moment when the keys were transferred the new mayor was taking the oath of office.

All England rejoiced; but across the water, in Germany, was a man who was not at all pleased to hear that a son and heir was born to Victoria, for he had always had a lingering hope that he might yet become King of Great Britain. His aide-de-camp said that King Ernest was generally ill-natured when he heard from England; and he was indignant enough when he was not asked to become his grandnephew's godfather. Who should be the chief sponsor was a weighty matter; but Baron Stockmar's advice was followed, and the King of Prussia was invited to take the place of honor. The Queen wished the little Prince named Albert for the husband who was so dear to her, and Edward for the father whom she could not remember, and these names were given him. This small Prince was an expensive baby, for it is said that the festivities at his christening cost at least $1,000,000. The Queen gave him the title of Prince of Wales when he was only a month old by signing an interesting bit of parchment which declared that she girded him with a sword and put a golden rod into his hands that he might direct and defend the land of the Welsh.

In all these regal honors and rejoicings the little baby sister was not forgotten, and the Queen wrote in her journal: "Albert brought in dearest little Pussy in such a smart merino dress, trimmed with blue, which mamma had given her, and a pretty cap. She was very dear and good."

The children's father and mother would have been very glad to forget all outside cares and splendors and live quietly by themselves, but that could not be. There was much to think of and many subjects concerning which they felt anxiety. One of these was the change of government, for a little before the birth of the Prince the event took place which the Queen had dreaded so long, the victory of the Tories and the resignation of Lord Melbourne. Never was a retiring Minister more generous to his opponents and more thoughtful of the comfort of his sovereign. Soon after his resignation he had a little conversation with Mr. Greville about the Tories.

"Have you any means of speaking to these chaps?" he asked.

"Certainly," answered Greville.

"I think there are one or two things Peel ought to be told," said Lord Melbourne, "and I wish you would tell him. When he wishes to propose anything, he must tell the Queen his reasons. She is not conceited; she knows there are many things which she does not understand, and she likes to have them explained."

Sir Robert was grateful for the advice; and followed it. It was not pleasant for him to become Prime Minister, for, although the Queen treated him with the utmost courtesy, he knew that she looked upon him as responsible for cutting down the grant to Prince Albert and for opposing her wish to give the Prince precedence next to herself. Peel had done exactly what he thought was right, but he could not help feeling sensitive when he was brought into so close relationship with the Queen and knew that this relationship was not welcome to her. "Any man with the feelings of a gentleman would be annoyed at having unavoidably given her so much pain," he said. Moreover, he was exceedingly shy, "so shy that he makes me shy," said the Queen. Fortunately, Sir Robert and Prince Albert found that they had much in common in their love for literature and art, and the Queen could not help liking the man who showed such warm appreciation of the husband whom she adored. Very soon Peel paid him a compliment that completely won her heart. The new houses of Parliament were to be decorated, and there was a strong desire felt by all who were interested in art that they should be so artistic as to be an honor to the country. Peel invited the Prince to become the chairman of the commission which was to control the matter. This position gave him the best of opportunities to become connected with the prominent men of the country, and both Prince and Queen were grateful to Peel for his thoughtfulness. The Queen came to appreciate the Tory Premier; then she saw that the Tories were not so black as they were painted; and before the end of 1841, Victoria was no longer "Queen of the Whigs," but Queen of all her people.

The Queen had no easy life. "She has most of the toil and least of the enjoyments of the world," wrote her husband. She had also much of the danger. Without an enemy in the world, she was shot at twice during the summer of 1842 by men who seemed to have no motive for such a deed. When Peel heard of the attempt on her life, he hurried to the palace to consult with the Prince. The Queen entered the room, and the shy, cold, self-contained Minister actually wept tears of joy at her safety. After that, there was no question about the friendliness between the Queen and her Premier.

Just how these would-be assassins should be punished was an important matter, and here the common sense of the sovereign found a way out of the dilemma. "It is a mistake," she said, "to treat such attempts as high treason, for it dignifies the crime, and makes the criminals feel that they are bold and daring

HOUSEKEEPING IN A PALACE

men." Parliament learned from her wisdom and passed a bill punishing any attempt upon the sovereign's life by imprisonment and flogging. This had so good an effect that the Queen saw seven years of peace before another attempt was made to injure her.

In spite of all these dangers and political responsibilities, Victoria was radiantly happy. The home life was all that she could have asked. She and the Prince were not only husband and wife, they were the best of comrades. Whenever they could win a little leisure from the cares of state, they read and sketched and sang together. Music gave them both the most intense pleasure, and both had rare musical ability, which had been carefully cultivated. Mendelssohn describes a visit to them which he seems to have enjoyed as much as they.

The great composer says that he found Prince Albert alone, but as they were looking at the new organ and trying the different stops, the Queen came in, wearing a very simple morning gown.

"I am glad that you have come," she said. "We love your music, and it is a great pleasure to have you with us."

"I thank your Majesty," replied the guest, and he went on to speak of the beauty of the organ.

"Yes, it is indeed fine," said the Queen, "but then I think any instrument fine when the Prince is playing on it. But what confusion!" she exclaimed, glancing around the room. The wind had scattered leaves of music over the floor, even on the pedals of the organ, and she knelt down and began to pick them up. Prince Albert and Mendelssohn started to help, but she said, "No, go on with the stops, and I will put things straight."

"Will you not play something for me?" begged Mendelssohn of the Prince, and added, "so I can boast about it in Germany?" The Prince played, while the Queen sat by him listening and looking perfectly happy. Then Mendelssohn played his chorus, "How Lovely Are the Messengers," but before he was at the end of the first verse, his royal hosts were singing with him.

"It is beautiful," said the Queen. "Have you written any new songs? I am very fond of your old ones."

"You ought to sing one for him?" suggested the Prince.

"If you only will," pleaded Mendelssohn.

"I will try the 'Frühling's Lied,'" she said, "if it is here, but I am afraid that all my music is packed to go to Claremont." Prince Albert went to look for it, but when he returned, he reported that it was already packed.

"But could it perhaps be unpacked?" suggested Mendelssohn daringly.

"It shall be," said the Queen. "We must send to Lady Frances." The bell was rung, and the servants were sent to find the music, but they were unsuccessful.

"I will go," the Queen declared, and she left the room. While she was gone, the Prince said: "She begs that you will accept this present as a remembrance," and he gave the composer a beautiful ring marked "V. R. 1842."

When the Queen returned, she said, "It is really most annoying; all my things are gone to Claremont."

"Please do not make me suffer for the accident," begged Mendelssohn, and at last another song was chosen. "She really sang it charmingly," he wrote in a letter, but when he told her so, she exclaimed, "Oh! if I only had not been so frightened."

The Prince sang, and Mendelssohn gave them one of his wonderful improvisations; then the musician took his leave. "But do come to England again soon and pay us a visit," said the Queen earnestly, as he made his farewells.

Running about to see the world was not so common an amusement in the first half of the nineteenth century as it is to-day, neither were railroads as common, and the Queen of England was twenty-three years of age before she ever made a journey by rail. This new way of traveling produced quite a disturbance among some of her attendants. The Master of Horse said that as it was his business to arrange for her journeys, he must assure himself that the engine was in proper condition; and, much to the amusement of the engineer, he appeared at the railway station several hours before the train was to start, that he might inspect the engine, as if it were a horse. There was even more difficulty in satisfying the claims of the coachman. "When the Queen travels, it is my business to drive for her," he declared; "therefore, I must at least be on the engine." He was permitted to ride on the pilot engine, but the dust and cinders made such havoc with his scarlet livery and his white gloves that he concluded not to press his claims quite so urgently in future.

This famous journey was only twenty-five minutes long, and in spite of the gorgeousness of crimson carpets laid from the royal carriage to the train, it could not have been especially comfortable, for airbrakes and good roadbeds were inventions yet to come. Nevertheless, the royal lady was not discouraged in her desire to travel, and in the autumn of 1842 she and the Prince made a journey to Scotland.

Much that she saw was almost as new to her as it would have been to any village maiden who had never left her home, and she was interested in whatever came before her. She was especially delighted with Edinburgh. "It is beautiful," she wrote; "totally unlike anything else I have ever seen." As she entered the city, she was met by the Royal Archers Bodyguard. This was an association formed by one of her royal ancestors more than two hundred years before. Its special business was to protect the sovereign, and in the old days its members were covered from head to foot with armor. Long before Victoria's time the armor had vanished, but in memory of the olden customs each man carried a bow in one hand and had arrows stuck through his belt. As soon as the Queen appeared, they began to perform their ancient office, walking close beside the carriage all the way through the town.

HOUSEKEEPING IN A PALACE

In this journey the Queen and Prince Albert were received by various noblemen, but the most picturesque greeting was at the home of Lord Breadalbane at Taymouth. As they drove up to the castle, the gates were thrown open, and there stood their host in a Highland dress, at the head of a company of Highlanders, who were gorgeous in the bright-colored tartan of the Campbells. Pipers were playing on the bagpipes, salutes were fired, the soldiers and the crowd of country folk cheered over and over again. When the royal guests went into the house and were escorted up the wide stone staircase, long lines of Highlanders in kilts stood on both sides of the hall and the stairway. It is no wonder that the Queen wrote in her journal that it seemed like the old feudal times. In the evening the gardens were illuminated. There were no electric lights then, but she says there was "a whole chain of lamps along the railing, and on the ground was written in lamps, 'Welcome, Victoria—Albert.'" Bonfires were kindled on the tops of the hills, and fireworks were set off. Then the bagpipes began to play, torches were brought on the lawn in front of the house, and by their wild and flaring light the Highlanders danced the gayest, merriest reels that can be imagined. The visitors spent several days in this charming place. A ball was given for them, but the Queen seems to have enjoyed much more heartily the quiet drives that she took about the country, the row up the lake, with two pipers sitting in the bow of the boat, piping and singing weird Gaelic boat songs; and perhaps most of all, the little picnics they had and the walks that they took, for there was no one to stare at them, and they roamed about in perfect freedom, guarded only by two Highlanders,

IN THE DAYS OF QUEEN VICTORIA

Queen Victoria—*From a portrait taken shortly after her marriage.*

who, according to the ancient custom, followed them with drawn swords wherever they went.

During the next two or three years, the Queen and Prince Albert seized every opportunity for travel, short though their journeys had to be. They visited not only several of the lordly mansions of England, but they also spent a few days in Belgium and made a short stay at the court of the French King. In 1844, they went again to Scotland, and this time "Vicky," as they called the Princess Royal, was old enough to go with them. There were two more children in the royal nursery by this time, and the Queen wrote in her journal that "Alice and the baby and good Bertie" came to bid the travelers farewell. She was quite delighted that "Vicky" stood at the window of a little inn and bowed to the people outside. One of her hosts on this visit to Scotland was the Duke of Argyll. She describes in her journal his son, the two-year old Marquis of Lorne, and calls him "such a merry, independent little child."

One of the disadvantages of being a sovereign is that the simplest acts are looked upon as being of political significance. Victoria wished to meet the French King, to whom Prince Albert was distantly related, and she did not wish to talk politics. On her visit to France she was interested in seeing the King's barge and its many oarsmen in white, with red sashes; in the royal chapel, the first Roman Catholic church that she had ever entered; in the little picnic that the King ordered in the forest; in the picturesque white caps of the peasant women, their bright-colored aprons and kerchiefs; and she noted even the tone of the church bells, and said that it was much prettier than that of the bells in

IN THE DAYS OF QUEEN VICTORIA

England. She enjoyed her visit heartily; but far away in Russia the keen-eyed Emperor Nicholas was watching her movements, and he was not quite pleased. "The government of Turkey will soon fall to pieces," he said to himself, "and if it does, France would like to secure a piece of that country. If England should help her, she might be able to do so, and this visit looks as if England and France were becoming too friendly." The result of the Czar's meditations was that word was sent to the Queen that he was on his way to visit her and might be looked for at once. Queen Victoria had expected him to come the following year, but he liked to make visits in this sudden fashion, and there was nothing to do but to prepare for him as best she could in forty-eight hours, for she had no longer time in which to make ready.

The Queen had not been especially anxious for the visit, she feared there would be "constraint and bustle;" but she soon found that quiet, simple ways of living were most pleasing to her guest, and she wrote to King Leopold, "He is very easy to get on with." His greatest interest was in military matters, and he was so much of a soldier that he said he felt without his uniform almost as if he had been skinned. He was taken to a review, of course, and this he thoroughly enjoyed. "Won't you allow me to ride down the line," he asked the Queen, "so I can see my old comrades?" Down the line he went, and was greeted everywhere with enthusiastic cheers. When the Duke of Wellington appeared, the crowd began to hurrah for him, for the man who had won the battle of Waterloo was the nation's idol. "Please don't, please don't," he said, riding

HOUSEKEEPING IN A PALACE

along close to the crowd. "Don't cheer for me; cheer for the Emperor."

This military Emperor had his own ideas about what the bed of a soldier should be, even if the soldier was at the head of an empire, and before he took possession of his bedroom at Windsor Castle, he had his camp-bed set up, and sent to the stables for straw to stuff the leathern case that formed his mattress.

The Emperor was delighted with his visit, and when the Queen invited him to come again, he said rather sadly: "You do not know how difficult it is for us to do such things." Then he kissed the royal children and the hand of the Queen, and made his farewells. The Queen kissed him, as sovereigns are expected to do at the beginning and end of a state visit, and the reception of the mighty Czar was over. "By living in the same house together quietly and unrestrainedly, I not only see these great people, but know them," said the Queen as simply as if she herself were not one of the "great people."

CHAPTER VIII

A HOME OF OUR OWN

IT is very delightful to live in palaces and entertain kings and emperors; but Queen Victoria's palaces belonged to the English nation, and not to herself, and, as has been said, their royal tenants had to suffer many inconveniences because they were not at liberty to manage their own housekeeping as they chose. "If we only had a home of our own!" said the Queen and Prince Albert to each other, and at last they decided to buy one. They talked the matter over with Sir Robert Peel, whom they had come to look upon as a faithful friend, and he told them of a beautiful estate which was for sale.

This property was situated on the Isle of Wight. It was far enough from London to assure them of privacy, and it was so near that there need be no delay in matters of government. In this charming place there were trees and valleys and hills, a wide stretch of sea-beach, with the woods growing almost to the water's edge; and, best of all, the royal family could walk and drive and wander about without feeling that they were on continual exhibition. There was a palace at Brighton which the Queen had sometimes occupied for the sake of being near the sea; but Brighton had become so much of a city, and the houses had clustered so closely about the palace, that there was no longer any view of the ocean from the lower windows, and no member of the royal family could go outside of the grounds without being followed by inquisitive crowds. At Osborne, as the new purchase was named, there was perfect freedom. Perhaps the "grown ups" of the household appreciated the liberty indoors quite as much as that out of doors, for here there were no "departments" to consult, and if a pane of glass was broken, there was no need of sending over the kingdom for the signatures of five men before it could be mended.

The house was pretty, but it was too small, and a new one had to be built. Prince Albert made all the plans for it, and he was as eager as the Queen to get into a home of their own. Nevertheless, even in his eagerness he did not forget the good of others. The longer the work of building and beautifying the grounds lasted, the better it was for the workmen; and so when harvest time came, he discharged large numbers of his men, saying: "Work in the fields now; then, when the harvest is in, come to me, and you shall have work here again."

The cost of the house came from the Queen's own purse, from the regular grant made her by Parliament, though most sovereigns have called upon the nation to build whatever dwellings they thought desirable. The people of the kingdom were pleased to hear the English Court called the most magnificent in Europe, and many statesmen expected that when a new palace was to be built or a royal guest to be entertained, the sovereign would ask Parliament for a special grant of money to pay the expense. Frequently far more was expected of members of the royal family than their purses could provide, and then came debts. King Leopold had not been able to live within his grant, and the Duke of Kent had left indebtedness at his death. The little Princess, who had not been allowed to buy a box until she had the money to pay for it, meant, now that she was on the throne, to carry out the principle on which she had been brought up. The first thing that she did was to pay her father's debts, and while living in as much splendor as her people desired, she managed her income so well that she could afford to build a palace if she chose. Prince Albert heartily approved of this wise economy, and he carried out the same plan in managing the farm of the new estate; he spent lavishly in improving the land, but unlike most "fancy farmers," he made his costly improvements so skillfully that they were paid for in the generous increase in crops.

When the new house was done, there was a joyful homecoming. As the Queen passed through the door, one of the maids of honor threw an old shoe after her, "to bring good luck," she said. To the Prince, entering into the new home brought memories of his childhood in Coburg, and after the first dinner he said, "We have a hymn in Germany for such occasions. It begins:

"Bless, O God, our going forth,
Bless Thou, too, our coming in."

A HOME OF OUR OWN

So it was that the new house was opened. Not only the grown folk, but the merry little company of princes and princesses, were very happy in it whenever a few days could be spared for its pleasures. As they grew older, a Swiss Cottage was built for them, and this was *their* house. There was a charming little kitchen with a cooking stove, so that the girls could try all sorts of experiments in the cooking line; and happy they were when they could persuade their father and mother to partake of a "banquet" of their own preparing. The boys had a forge and a carpenter's bench, where they built small boats and chairs and tables and wheelbarrows. Every child had a garden, and there he raised not only flowers, but fruit and vegetables. In this little paradise the children did what they liked, but they were shown the best way of doing it. A gardener taught them how to manage their gardens, and whenever their vegetables were a success, they either gave them away or sold them at market price to the royal kitchen. Prince Albert himself taught the boys how to use tools, and helped them to begin a museum of insects, minerals, and all sorts of curiosities, like the one that he and his brother Ernest had had in Coburg when they were boys.

Not only at Osborne, but wherever the royal children were, they were brought up as simply as the Queen herself had been. Whatever material was bought for their clothes had to be shown to the Queen, and if it was rich or expensive, she would refuse to allow it to be used. As soon as the princes and princesses were old enough, they were taught to take as much care of their clothes as if they had been a poor man's children. One of their nurses wrote that they had "quite poor living—only a bit of roast beef and perhaps a plain pudding;" and she added, "The Queen is as fit to have been a poor man's wife as a queen." Baron Stockmar was consulted on all nursery questions, and he said that it was more difficult to manage a nursery than a kingdom.

The Queen tried to make her children understand that they were no better than other children just because they were princes or princesses, and they were obliged to behave with perfect courtesy to the servants of the palace as well as to kings and emperors. It is said that once upon a time two of the children thought it very amusing to take possession of the brushes and blacken the face of a woman who was cleaning a stove; but when the Queen mother discovered their prank, she took the small culprits by the hand and led them to the woman's room and made them apologize most humbly. The little Princess Royal "Vicky" was so independent a young lady that she would sometimes break through her mother's teachings. The story is told that one day a sailor lifted her on board the royal yacht, saying as he sat her down, "There you are, my little lady." "I'm a princess, I'm not a little lady," the child retorted; but the watchful mother was listening, and she said, "That is true. Tell the kind sailor that you are not a little lady yet, but that you hope to be some day." Occasionally this willful little Princess preferred to bear a punishment rather than give up her own way. The Queen and the Prince addressed Dr. Brown as "Brown," and the small child followed their example. "You will be sent to bed if you do that again," said the

A HOME OF OUR OWN

Queen, but the next morning when Dr. Brown appeared, the little girl said with special distinctness: "Good morning, Brown, and good night, Brown, for I'm going to bed, Brown," and, with her saucy little head high in the air, she marched off to bed.

Happy as the Queen and the Prince were in their home life, one subject in connection with her husband always troubled the loving wife, and that was the annoying question of precedence. She wrote of him in her journal: "He is above me in everything really, and therefore I wish that he should be equal in rank to me." In England she could "put the Prince where she wished him to be," but Parliament had given him no rank, and therefore out of England some sovereigns, like King Ernest, positively refused to grant him any honors that were not due to the younger son of the Duke of Coburg; and when precedence was accorded him, the Queen had to express gratitude as for a personal favor to herself. Unknown to the Prince, she had a long talk on the subject with Baron Stockmar.

"I wish him to have the title of King Consort," she said earnestly.

"A king consort without the authority of a king would be a novelty," replied the Baron, "and the English people do not like anything for which there is no precedent. Queen Anne's husband was never called king."

"But Queen Anne's husband was stupid and insignificant," declared the Queen. "There has never been a case like ours before. Albert and I reign together. He is sovereign as much as I. We discuss all matters and decide together."

"True," admitted the Baron, "but the constitution does not provide for such a condition of affairs. I will talk with Peel about it."

Peel felt as Stockmar did, that it was not wise to propose such a title. The subject arose again some years later, and the shrewd Baron wrote to the Prince in his usual straightforward fashion: "Never abandon your firm, powerful position to run after butterflies. You have the substance; stick by it." The title was never given him, but it was true that he had "the substance." The Queen no longer met her Ministers alone; the Prince was always with her to help and suggest. Whenever either she or the Prince spoke to the Council, the word "I" was not used; it was always "We think so-and-so should be done."

Not only the Council but the whole country were gaining in knowledge of the Prince's wisdom and devotion to the good of the kingdom, and in 1847 a valued mark of appreciation was given him in his election as Chancellor of the University of Cambridge, one of the greatest honors that could have been bestowed upon him. The Queen was delighted, because she knew that the position was not given out of compliment to her, but was something that he himself had earned. Soon after the election, came the installation. The magistrates and Yeomanry went to the station to meet the Queen, and then marched before her into the town. She was escorted into the Great Hall of Trinity College and led to an armchair which stood on a platform under a canopy. Soon after she had seated herself, the new Chancellor entered at the farther end of the hall, followed by the long line of university dignitaries. He wore a robe of black and gold, so long that it had to be held up by two gentlemen. When he stood in front of the armchair that represented the throne, he made a low bow and delivered his address. "The situation was almost absurd for us," said the Queen afterwards, but the Prince read his with perfect command of his countenance, and the Queen was quite serious until she caught his eye for a moment at the end of the speech. She half smiled, but in an instant she was again the dignified sovereign, and she declared with a little emphasis that brought forth shouts of applause, "The choice which the university has made of a Chancellor has my most entire approbation."

Not long afterwards the new Chancellor and his royal wife paid another visit to Cambridge. It was a little muddy, and the Queen hesitated a moment before getting out of the carriage. Instantly one of the students threw his gown upon the ground for her to step on, and others followed his example.

When Victoria thought of her husband and her children, she was supremely happy, but when she thought of the different kingdoms of Europe, and even of her own realm, there was much in 1847 and 1848 to make her unhappy. All Europe was restless and uneasy. Revolt had broken out in Italy, France, Germany, and other countries. The reigning sovereigns in most of these kingdoms were related to her either by blood or by marriage, and she could but feel grief for their trials, and, in some instances, fear for their safety. Indeed, the King and Queen of France had to flee to England, and they spent the remainder of their lives at Claremont. In Victoria's own realm there was trouble. Ireland was suffering from a terrible famine. Thousands of Irish were dying of either starvation or fever. In England there was no starvation, but everyone felt the hard times more or less. Those who had money did not dare to invest it, because business was so unsettled that they were afraid of loss. As capital was not invested, there was little work to be had, and the poor suffered severely. The rich as well as the poor felt the general stagnation. Greville said that his income was only half the usual amount, and even in royal palaces strict economy was practiced.

There was a special reason for great uneasiness in London. According to the laws at that time, no one could become a member of the House of Commons who did not own land enough to receive from it an annual income of $1500. This law had been made in the belief that a man who owned land would be more interested in the welfare of his country than a man who had none. Thousands of workingmen were not allowed even to vote. When work was plenty, and they were comfortable and busy, they did not think so much about their rights; but when work failed, they began to say to one another: "This is all the fault of the laws. If everyone could vote, and if poor men as well as rich men could become members of Parliament, laws would be made for the good of the whole nation and not merely for the landowners."

These men held meetings to discuss such matters, and they concluded to send in a petition to Parliament, setting forth their wrongs and demanding that changes should be made. The plan was explained in what was called the People's Charter, and therefore its supporters were spoken of as Chartists.

No one would have objected to having as many petitions sent to Parliament as the house would hold, but among the people were many hot-headed persons who had much to say about "oppression" and "revolution." The crowds sometimes became noisy and turbulent, and one evening some of them rushed wildly toward Buckingham Palace. The only harm that they did was to break some street lamps; and when their leader was arrested by the police, he made no resistance, but began to cry. Nevertheless, people felt very uneasy, and when it was reported that on the 10th of April the petition would be presented by 1,000,000 men, there was much alarm in the city. Shops were barricaded, weapons were put where they could be caught up in a moment, and old muskets that had not been used for half a century were brought down from the garrets and put in order for the riots that were feared. The Duke of Wellington, as commander-in-chief of the army, made very wise preparations. There was no display of soldiers or cannon, but Buckingham Palace and the public buildings were quietly filled with armed men, and gun-boats were brought up the river. The Queen had shown again and again that she was no coward, and she would have stayed in London, but her Ministers persuaded her to take her three-weeks'-old baby to Osborne House. All London trembled when the 10th of April arrived; but when night came, those who had feared most laughed heartiest. The whole affair had ended in a few thousand men starting for Parliament with the petition. "You cannot cross the bridge in mass," said the police, and the Chartists went home meekly, sending their petition in cabs.

The Queen had long wished to go to Ireland, and in 1849 she and the Prince and the four older children went to that country in the yacht *Victoria and Albert*. Now, however indignant the Irish might be at England's rule of their country, they would not give the Queen any but the most cordial greeting; and when the yacht sailed into the mouth of the River Lee, the people of the place called Cove of Cork asked that she would step ashore, if only for a moment. "We wish to change the name of our town," they said, "so that it may mark the place where the Queen first set her foot on Irish soil." The flag was run up on which was written the word "Cove," but as soon as the Queen had gone back to the yacht, the flag was dropped, and another was run up marked "Queenstown."

The *Victoria and Albert* went on to Cork, and the party also visited several other places in Ireland. Wherever they went, the crowds pressed to the water's edge with cheering and shouts of welcome. Cannon were fired and bells were set to ringing. Every little cottage had its flag, or at least a wreath of flowers and evergreens. All were interested in the royal children, and at Kingstown an old lady cried out: "Oh! Queen dear, make one of them Prince Patrick, and all Ireland will die for you."

When the Irish visit had come to its end, and the Queen was about to leave for England, the crowds

A HOME OF OUR OWN

on the shore cheered her more wildly than ever, and both the Queen and the Prince climbed the paddlebox and waved their handkerchiefs again and again. "Go slowly," ordered the Queen, and the boat moved very slowly along, keeping close to the pier. The crowds cheered with more enthusiasm than before, and three times a return was given to their salute by lowering the royal standard. One of the Queen's party said: "There is not an individual in the town who does not take the Queen's going on the paddlebox and lowering the royal standard as a personal compliment to himself."

The year following the visit to Ireland the Queen's seventh child was born, a boy.

"Now we are just as many as the days of the week," cried the brothers and sisters joyfully.

"But which of us shall be Sunday?" asked one.

"The new baby," answered Princess "Vicky" decidedly, "because he's just come, and we must be polite to him and give him the best."

The little boy was named Patrick, as the old woman in Ireland had suggested, but his first name was Arthur, for the Duke of Wellington, on whose eighty-first birthday he was born.

The days of the Queen were full of joys and sorrows that came almost hand in hand. Her home life was perfectly happy, but her duties as a sovereign took much time that she would have gladly given to her family. "It is hard," she said, "that I cannot always hear my children say their prayers." She had the warmest, most devoted friends, but in the six years preceding

1850, she had lost several who could never be replaced. Sir Robert Peel and Lord Melbourne had died, the opposing Ministers who had both won her confidence and gratitude; and the "good Queen Adelaide," who had loved the little Princess Victoria as if she had been her own child, was also gone. The sorrow which Prince Albert felt at the loss of his father had been to his wife a grief almost as deep; and both she and the Prince were saddened by the loss of the Coburg grandmother, who loved him so that she was almost heartbroken on his leaving her to make his home in England, and called piteously after his carriage, "Oh, Albert, Albert!" The three who had been nearest to the Queen in her childhood were living, her mother, Dr. Davys, and Baroness Lehzen. The kind, scholarly clergyman she had made Bishop of Peterborough, and she saw him from time to time. After the marriage of the Queen the Baroness Lehzen returned to her friends in Germany, but the busy sovereign found time to send her long and frequent letters.

The losses of the Queen were many, but with Prince Albert by her side, she felt that she could bear whatever came; and it was a great happiness to her that the better he was known in the country, the more highly the nation thought of him. They could hardly help esteeming him, for he seemed never to have a thought of himself; all was for the Queen and for her people. For several years he had had a plan in his mind for a great industrial exhibition. When he first laid the scheme before the public, the people were wildly enthusiastic. Then, as the difficulties arose, there was much criticism. The building would cost $1,000,000, and subscriptions were slow. *Punch* brought out a cartoon inscribed, "Please to remember the Exposition." It represented a boy holding out his cap for pennies. Under the picture was written:

> "Pity the sorrows of a poor young Prince—
>   Whose costly scheme has borne him to your door;
> Who's in a fix—the matter not to mince—
>   Oh, help him out, and commerce swell your store."

Prince Albert laughed heartily at the cartoon, added it to his collection, and worked all the harder for the exposition.

There was much opposition to admitting foreign exhibits, for many English manufacturers had a wild fancy that the sight of them would prevent the English from patronizing home products. "All the villains of the Continent will be here," declared the grumblers. "They will murder the Queen and begin a revolution." In Parliament, one of the members invoked the lightning to fall from heaven and destroy the half-finished building. Nevertheless, enormous masses of goods were constantly arriving, and the mighty structure continued to rise. It was made of iron and glass, and was like an enormous greenhouse. Thackeray wrote of it:

> "And see, 'tis done!
> As though 'twere by a wizard's rod,
> A blazing arch of lucid glass
> Leaps like a fountain from the grass
>   To meet the sun."

IN THE DAYS OF QUEEN VICTORIA

The Crystal Palace, the people called it, and no better name could have been given. It stretched out one thousand feet in length, and part of it was one hundred feet high, so high that two elm trees which had been growing on its site grew on in freedom under its glass roof. The iron-work was painted a clear, bright blue. There were scarlet hangings, fountains, statues, banners, tapestries, flowers, palms, everything that could make it bright and beautiful.

May 1, 1851, had been named as the day of opening. In the royal family the day began with birthday gifts for the little Arthur—toys from the parents, a clock from the Duchess of Kent, and, strange presents for a baby, a bronze statuette and a beautiful paper-knife, from the Prince and Princess of Prussia. Long before noon, the Queen, the Prince, and the two older children drove to Crystal Palace. As they entered, there was a flourish of trumpets, followed by tremendous cheering. The Queen was radiant with happiness as she walked down the broad aisle with her husband. She wore a pink silk dress of Irish poplin, and on her head was a diamond tiara. She led by the hand the Prince of Wales, a bright, handsome little fellow. The Princess Royal wore a white dress, and on her head was a wreath of roses. She held her father's hand. The cheers grew louder and louder, then the deep tones of the organ broke in upon them. The music of two hundred instruments and six hundred voices followed, leading the thousands present in the National Hymn. After this the Prince left the side of the Queen, and, returning at the head of the commissioners, he read her the formal report. She made a short reply. The Archbishop of Canterbury offered up prayer, and the wonderful "Hallelujah Chorus" resounded through the lofty arches. While this was being sung, a Chinese mandarin, who had been walking about most perfectly at his ease and quite indifferent to the gazing crowds, now took his stand before the Queen and made a very profound obeisance. He proved to be of considerable use a little later, for when the long procession of distinguished Englishmen and foreigners was formed, it occurred to someone that China was not represented, and the dignified mandarin was taken possession of as an addition to the train. He made no objections, but marched along with his former tranquility, thinking apparently that all foreigners were treated in such manner by those remarkable people, the Englishmen.

The Duke of Wellington was in the procession, and the walk around the building was to him a triumphal progress, for the women waved their handkerchiefs and kissed their hands, while the men cheered and shouted, "The Duke! The Duke!" In the midst of all his glory, he did not forget his little year-old namesake and godson; and later in the day, his eighty-second birthday, he called at Buckingham Palace with a golden cup and some toys of his own selection for the little boy.

So ended what Victoria called "the proudest and happiest day of my life, a thousand times superior to the coronation." In her journal she wrote: "Albert's name is immortalized. God bless my dearest Albert, God bless my dearest country!"

CHAPTER IX

NIS! NIS! NIS! HURRAH!

FEW men in England worked as hard as Prince Albert, the uncrowned King. If a corner stone of a school, a hospital, or a public building was to be laid, a missionary society to be formed, some new docks to be founded, a museum to be opened, Prince Albert must be present. He must attend naval reviews, councils to discuss reforms at Cambridge, dinners of scientific men, and first meetings of societies to aid superannuated servants. He must not only be seen, but he must be heard, for he was expected to make a speech on every occasion. In fact, whenever he opened the door of his own rooms, some delegation seemed to be waiting to ask him to attend a meeting and make a speech.

All these demands upon his time took him away from the Queen, and every absence made her lonely. She wrote to King Leopold: "You cannot think how forlorn I am when he is away; all the numerous children are as nothing. It seems as if the whole light of the house and home were gone." Prince Albert never let a day pass during any of these absences without writing to her. Once when he went to an important

NIS! NIS! NIS! HURRAH!

meeting of scientific men, he sent back the same day a little note that said: "I have locked myself in to send you two lines as a token of my life and love. You will be feeling somewhat lonely and forsaken among the two and a half millions of human beings in London, and I too feel the want of only one person to give a world of life to everything around me." The following day he sent her another letter, although it could reach her only two hours before his own arrival. However pressing his business might be, he always found time to write a word to her. One of these notes read:

"Your faithful husband, agreeably to your wishes, reports:

"1. That he is still alive;

"2. That he has discovered the North Pole from Lincoln Cathedral, but without finding either Captain Ross or Sir John Franklin;

"3. That he has arrived at Brocklesby, and received the address;

"4. That he subsequently rode out, and got home quite covered with snow, and with icicles on his nose;

"5. That the messenger is waiting to carry off this letter, which you will have in Windsor by the morning;

"6. Last, not least (in the dinner-speeches' phrase), that he loves his wife, and remains her devoted husband."

In the midst of all these engagements, the home life and the education of the children were not neglected. Lord Melbourne and Baron Stockmar had been consulted in regard to tutors and nursery arrangements as earnestly as on important political actions. Bishop Davys lived so simply that the Queen could not disturb him by a royal visit, but whenever she passed through Peterborough, she had her train delay so that he could come to her, and she could talk with him about the children and have his advice in regard to their training and their future. Lessons were important matters in the royal family, and if the governess was ill, either the Queen or the Prince heard the children recite, so that there should be no loss. There is a story that when a clergyman, who was hearing them say the catechism, remarked, "Your governess has taught you very thoroughly," they cried, "Oh, mamma always teaches us our catechism." She was interested in every detail of their lives, and when the man who made the clothes of the sailors on the *Victoria and Albert* made a tiny sailor suit for the little Prince of Wales, she seemed as pleased as if one suit a year was the limit of the royal purse.

Besides the calls of home and state, many other responsibilities fell upon the sovereign of England. In the latter part of 1851, trade was very dull in London, and the Queen decided to give a great fancy ball at Buckingham Palace so that sales might be increased. All the guests were asked to come in the costume of the time of the Stuarts, and this was so gay and picturesque that the ballroom must have been a most brilliant sight. The Queen wore a *gray dress*, but it was hardly as simple as one would expect from those two words, for it was glittering with gold and silver lace,

NIS! NIS! NIS! HURRAH!

Queen Victoria with her children,
King Edward and the Princess Royal.

while clusters of diamonds flashed forth from bows of rose-colored ribbon. The front of the dress opened to display a cloth-of-gold stomacher and underskirt made gorgeous with large emeralds. Strings of pearls were braided in with her hair, and upon her head she wore a small crown of diamonds and emeralds. Her gloves and shoes were heavily embroidered with gold. The costume of the Prince was a veritable rainbow, for he was all aglow in an orange coat, with its sleeves turned up with crimson velvet, breeches of crimson velvet, and stockings of lavender silk. This was not all by any means, for there were pink epaulets, pink satin bows, gold lace, a silver baldric, and a hat with long white ostrich feathers.

The Queen and the Prince retained their seats while the guests entered, each one making a low bow in passing. No one would have thought a royal ball complete without "the Duke," and he appeared in the dress of a Stuart general, his scarlet coat adorned with gold lace and point lace, and its sleeves slashed with white satin. Blue velvet trunks, crimson silk sash, white hat with blue plumes, and gold lace wherever there was room for it, completed his costume. So much he would concede to the state ball, but he utterly refused to appear in the long curls of the Stuart period, and in spite of all his gay trappings, he was still the stern old commander.

Another great ball given by the Lord Mayor of London followed this one, and it is no wonder that Queen and Prince were glad to leave London for a little rest. This time and many other times they went to Scotland. They loved Osborne, but the Prince was feeling the strain of his intense work, and the physicians thought that the air of the mountains would be better for him than that of the sea. Therefore they went to Balmoral, a charming little gray castle that they had bought. It stood on the banks of the swiftly flowing River Dee, in the midst of hills and forests. The life at Balmoral was far more simple than that of many non-royal families. Of course a Cabinet Minister was always in attendance, and messengers with boxes of state dispatches were continually coming and going; but there was much greater freedom than the Queen could enjoy elsewhere. In the early years at Balmoral, the English court consisted of the Queen, the Prince, their four children, the two teachers, and four other persons, secretaries and ladies in attendance.

At Balmoral they climbed mountains, searched for crystals and cairngorms, took long walks through the woods, made little picnics far up in the hills and built a cairn, or great pile of stones, each person placing one in turn, to mark the new ownership of the place. At dinner, the Prince wore the Scotch dress, and the Queen often wore over her shoulder a scarf of Stuart plaid. While the Prince was out shooting in the morning, she frequently ran about among the cottages, chatting easily and comfortably with the cottagers, comparing the height and weight of the latest royal baby with the latest baby of the neighborhood, going to the little stores in the village to buy dresses for poor people and toys for their children. On Sunday she went to the kirk like a true Scotchwoman, and one day she wrote in her journal enthusiastic praise of Dr. McLeod's sermons, because they were so "simple and eloquent," she said. She was never pleased to have a minister pay her any special attention in his sermons; she liked to have him look upon her as only one more of his people; but she wrote that when Dr. McLeod prayed for her and the Prince, and then said "Bless their children," it gave her "a lump in the throat."

In their everyday life the royal family were Scotch when they were in Scotland. The English children of the palace wore kilts and tartans, they played in the brooks with the Scotch children of the cottages; and the Princess Royal of England walked into a wasps' nest and met the same fate that would have befallen any little Scotch girl who had done the same thing. A Highland dancing master and a fiddler were engaged to come to Balmoral and teach the Queen and her court how to dance Scottish reels and strathspeys. One evening, after an early dinner, the court set off for a fourteen-mile drive to see a Scotch ball at a neighboring castle. It must have been a weird and beautiful sight. The dancing floor was out of doors, and all around it stood Highlanders in their gay plaids, holding blazing torches, while seven pipers provided the music. One of the reels was danced by eight Highlanders, each bearing a torch. Another interesting sight was the sword dance. In this two swords crossed were laid upon the ground, and the performer must dance around them without touching them.

As in the case of Osborne, it was soon apparent that the pretty little gray castle was not large enough for the Queen's housekeeping. "Every bed in the house was full," wrote Mr. Greville when he had been spending a night at Balmoral. A new house was de-

NIS! NIS! NIS! HURRAH!

cided upon, and when the corner stone was laid, there was one of the little family celebrations that were so delightful to both Queen and Prince. The sun shone brightly on the stone, as it hung over the place that it was to occupy. The servants of the castle stood in a semicircle on one side, and the workmen behind them. The royal family and their guests came out of the house together and took their places on the opposite side. A clergyman offered up a prayer for a blessing on the work and on the new home. A parchment giving the date on which the stone was laid was signed by every member of the royal family and put into a bottle, together with the current coins of the country. The bottle was sealed and placed in the cavity; the architect gave the Queen a trowel to spread the mortar; and the stone was lowered. The Queen then struck the stone with a mallet, and said: "I now declare that this corner stone is laid." She poured oil upon it in token of plenty, and wine in token of gladness; the pipers played; the workmen had a feast and a dance; and the new house was begun.

When the house was partly done, the builder came to Prince Albert and said:

"The price of materials has risen so greatly that keeping this contract will ruin me."

"Tell me just what the prices are now and what they were when we made the contract," said the Prince. The builder made a rapid list and gave it to him.

A few days later, the Prince sent for the builder and said:

"I find that you are right, and so I have burned my copy of the contract. I will be the builder myself, and if you will superintend the work of building, I will pay you the same amount that you expected to make on the contract."

Only a few days after one of the simple, merry evenings at Balmoral, a telegram broke into the happiness of the household, saying that the Duke of Wellington was dead. "One cannot think of this country without the Duke," wrote the Queen. "Not an eye will be dry. He was Britain's pride, her glory, her hero, the greatest man she had ever produced." A public funeral was given him by order of Parliament. His body lay in state in a great hall whose walls were heavily draped with black, relieved only by the banners that he had captured in battle. Guardsmen as motionless as statues stood at intervals along the passage, leaning upon their muskets, which rested, muzzles down, on the floor. On the coffin lay the Duke's sword and his cocked hat, and around the bier stood officers on guard, whose scarlet uniforms shone out of the darkness in the light of the tall wax candles that outlined the bier. Finally the body of the Duke was borne to St. Paul's on an iron gun-carriage, followed by the dead commander's horse with its empty saddle and by a long line of soldiers representing every regiment. Thousands of people lined the street through which the funeral *cortège* marched. They stood with bared heads and in such perfect silence that not a sound was heard but the steady tramp of feet and the roll of the funeral drums. So it was that the great soldier was buried amid the grief of the nation.

NIS! NIS! NIS! HURRAH!

Never was he needed more, for the sound of war was coming near. The Emperor Nicholas, whom the Queen had called so "easy to get along with," proved to be somewhat less easy than he had been when on a visit. He had declared that he should protect the Christians in Turkey from the outrages of the Turks; but France and England believed that what he was really aiming at was to get possession of Constantinople. If he succeeded in this, no ship could enter the Black Sea against his will, and it would not be impossible for him to gain control of the Asiatic lands then ruled by Great Britain. If this came to pass, Russia would be far more powerful than any other state in Europe. This was the belief of England and France, and they wished to oppose him.

The Queen was always against war, but when it was finally declared, early in 1854, she did everything in her power for the success of England. When the first regiments that were ready to go to the Crimea marched through the courtyard of Buckingham Palace, she and the Prince stood on the balcony as enthusiastic as the troops. Then she hastened to Osborne to say farewell to the warships that were starting for the Baltic. Prince Alfred had already made up his mind to be a sailor, and the Duke's little namesake was destined to follow the Duke's example and be a soldier, but they were as yet only small children, and the Queen exclaimed, "How I wish I had two sons in the army now and two in the navy!" Nothing that affected the war was too great or too small for her to notice, and she had a definite opinion on every subject.

"Your Majesty," said Lord Aberdeen, the Prime Minister, "it is proposed to have a day of humiliation and fasting for the success of our arms."

"I approve most heartily of a day of prayer," declared the Queen, "but not of calling it a day of humiliation. We are not humiliated. It is not our wickedness, but the selfish ambition and want of honesty of the Emperor which have brought on this war. We believe that our cause is just, and that we are contending for what is right."

"But it has long been the custom to call such days times of fasting and prayer," the Prime Minister suggested.

"We will thank God for the blessings we have enjoyed," said the Queen, "and ask His help and protection, but it is my particular wish that we call the day one of prayer and supplication."

The war was begun, and during the two years following, no one in the land suffered more intensely than the Queen. A powerful nation is always inclined to expect that its enemies may be crushed at a blow, but Russia was not so easily crushed.

The Queen was prepared for battles lost and battles won, but not for blunders and poor management; and to a woman as prompt and as careful of details as she, such faults were unpardonable. Before many months came the report of the Charge of the Light Brigade, which Tennyson has made famous in his poem. This useless charge by which six hundred men were sent to attack an army was caused by a mistake. "Someone had blundered." Thousands of copies of the poem were printed and sent to the soldiers who were besieging Sebastopol.

The Queen was in constant anxiety. Telegrams were false and misleading, and if one brought good news in the morning, she dared not rejoice lest it should be contradicted before night. It was then that the work of the "special correspondent" began, for a physician who was at the scene of the war sent letters to the *London Times*, and for the first time, the people at home knew the daily life of their soldiers.

The story told in the columns of the *Times* was a narration of terrible suffering, which was all the worse because so much of it was unnecessary. It does not seem possible that such stupid blunders could have been made. Food was sent that was not fit to eat. A whole shipload of much-needed shoes braved the storms of the Atlantic and Mediterranean—and proved to be all for the left foot! Clothes, blankets, and medicines in generous quantities lay in the holds of English vessels off Balaklava Bay, while men were dying for the lack of them. Shiploads of cattle arrived at Balaklava, and instead of being driven to the front, where there was sore need of beef, they were killed at once, and then came a long delay in arranging for transportation. The trouble was that it was no one's business to transport the stores, and no one had the right to interfere. The hospitals were so inefficient that nine-tenths of the men who died, perished of disease and mismanagement, and not from the bullets of the Russians.

IN THE DAYS OF QUEEN VICTORIA

When such news as this reached England, the whole country was aroused, but it was helpless. There was no time to change the organization of the conflicting "departments," and the Minister of War finally decided to do exactly what the Romans used to do in times of great difficulty: he appointed a dictator, with full power to go to the Crimea and do precisely as she thought best in making arrangements for the sick and wounded soldiers. This dictator was a woman named Florence Nightingale. She had a large fortune and a beautiful home, but she cared more for helping the sick than for living in luxury. For more than ten years she had been studying nursing, not only in England, but in France and Germany. Late in 1854 she went to the Crimea, taking forty-two nurses with her. It was no small task that she had undertaken, for in a short time ten thousand sick men were in her charge. The sanitary arrangements of the camp and the hospital were all in her hands. She was a gentle, modest woman, by nature shy and retiring, but where the comfort of her soldiers was concerned, she would never yield a point to anyone. "She had a voice of velvet and a will of steel," they said of her; and as she walked down the long aisles of the hospitals—in one of them the rows of beds stretched along for nearly two and a half miles—the poor sufferers kissed her very shadow. It was of her that Longfellow wrote

> "And slow, as in a dream of bliss,
> The speechless sufferer turns to kiss
> Her shadow, as it falls
> Upon the darkening walls."

NIS! NIS! NIS! HURRAH!

Meanwhile, the Queen was doing all in her power for the soldiers and their families. A Patriotic Fund was begun, and it soon reached $5,000,000. The "Soldier's Daughter" and her older girls sewed and knit for the army, the Prince of Wales, who was now thirteen years of age, painted a picture to be sold for the fund—no small contribution, for it brought nearly three hundred dollars—and the two older Princesses talked, as they sat knitting, about Miss Nightingale, and wished they could go to the Crimea and work by her side. At the opening of Parliament, the Queen began her speech bravely, but when she spoke of the war, her self-control failed her, and she struggled through the sentences as best she could with her eyes full of tears.

News of victories came, but nothing could be decisive except the capture of Sebastopol. "If we could only take Sebastopol!" she was always saying to herself, and one of her children said to a general who was starting for the Crimea, "Do hurry and take Sebastopol, or it will kill mamma." In September, 1855, the royal family and the Duchess of Kent were at Balmoral, when late one evening on the third day after their arrival, two telegrams were brought in, one for the Queen, and one for the Cabinet Minister.

"Good news," exclaimed the Queen. "This tells the details of the destruction of the Russian ships."

"But I have still better news," said the Minister. "Mine reads, 'Sebastopol is in the hands of the allies.' "

"Come and light the bonfire," cried Prince Albert, and he started up Craig Gowan, the hill opposite the house, where material for a bonfire had been piled up nearly a year before in the hope that Sebastopol would fall before the Queen had to return to London.

The gentlemen of the court hastened after the Prince, in full evening dress as they were. The little Princes were awakened and hurriedly dressed, and they followed after their father. The servants followed, the keepers, the workmen, the whole population of the village. The fires blazed out and shone on all the peaks round about. The people in the valleys knew what it meant, and they too hurried to the top of the hill. There was cheering, dancing, shouting, playing of bagpipes, and firing of guns. "It was a veritable witches' dance," declared the Prince when he came down. He was soon followed by the rest of the people, and when they were under the Queen's window, they sang to the music of the bagpipes, they fired guns, and then they cheered the Queen, the Prince, the Emperor of France, and last they gave a deafening "Nis! nis! nis! hurrah, for the fall of Sebastopol!"

It would seem as if this was excitement enough for one month, but four days later, the young Prince Frederick William of Prussia came to Balmoral to make a visit; and before the visit had lasted two weeks, there was a pretty little scene on the mountain side when he gave Princess "Vicky" a piece of white heather, the emblem of good fortune, and contrived to make it clear to her that the best fortune which could happen to him would be the gift of her hand. A few days before this, the father and mother and their guest had agreed that nothing should be said to the Princess for six months, but the secret had found its way out.

NIS! NIS! NIS! HURRAH!

The Princess Victoria had always been Baron Stockmar's special favorite, and she as well as her father wrote their good friend at once, and sent him the news that the kindly old matchmaker had been waiting for since the Princess was a little child, for such a marriage would make a strong alliance between England and Prussia, the two great Protestant powers of Europe. Prince Albert wrote, "The Prince is really in love, and the little lady does her best to please him. Come to us soon. We have so much to talk over." A little later, he wrote again of his hope that he should soon hear the children say, "Do you know, papa, that the Baron is in his room below?" He closed, "We positively must have some talk face to face."

The Princess was to be confirmed in the spring, and until that event was past, nothing was to be said in public of the engagement. The marriage was not to take place until at least a year after the confirmation, but Prince Albert felt that the time was far too short for the preparation that her future position would make desirable; and, busy man as he was, he set apart an hour every evening to talk with her on historical topics, and listen to the papers which she prepared on subjects that he had given her. In the spring came her confirmation, which was preceded by an examination in the catechism held in the presence of her father and mother, the Duchess of Kent, and the Archbishop of Canterbury.

This betrothal of the eldest daughter brought to the Queen mingled feelings of pleasure and pain; pleasure, because the alliance with Prussia, so desirable an arrangement for both countries, was to be brought about by a marriage that promised the happiness of her daughter; pain, because that marriage was the first break in the family circle. Nevertheless, in joy or in sorrow, the public life of the sovereign must go on. Many of the soldiers who had been severely wounded were sent home. The Queen had often visited them in the hospitals, and one day she said to her Minister:

"Those brave men ought to have medals that they can hand down to their children, and I have ordered a number to be made."

As the day appointed for the distribution of the medals drew near, the Minister asked if she would have them sent to the men.

"No," replied the Queen with decision, "I want to put those medals into their hands myself. I feel as if those men were my own children."

It was a pitiable company of sufferers that she met. There were men with deep red scars, men with empty sleeves, men tottering up to her on crutches to touch the hand of their Queen. Many of them would not give up their medals to be marked with their names, lest they should not receive again the very ones that the Queen had given them. One man was wheeled up in a chair. He had lost one leg and the foot from the other, but he had refused to give up the command of his battery till the fight was over, and had given his orders as calmly as if he had not been touched.

"Such bravery as that," cried the Queen, with tears in her eyes, "calls for more than a medal, and you shall be one of my aides-de-camp."

NIS! NIS! NIS! HURRAH!

"That pays me amply for everything," he replied. The Queen wrote the account of this incident to King Leopold. "One must revere and love such soldiers as those," she added.

She was never weary of visiting the hospitals and camps. As the regiments returned from the Crimea in the spring and summer of 1856, there were reviews without end. On one occasion she reviewed eighteen thousand troops. She was dressed in the uniform of a field marshal, with a dark blue skirt; and as she rode down the front and returned by the rear, the thousands of men presented arms, and the bands of twenty regiments gave her a joyful greeting. Then she rode to a little mound from which she watched her troops as they filed past her.

There was no limit to the enthusiasm and loyalty which were aroused by the presence of the Queen. One review was held in a pelting rain. The evolutions were spoiled, and the men had every reason to feel gloomy and disappointed, but the Queen saved the day, for she rose in her carriage and made them a warm-hearted little speech of welcome that was like a flash of sunshine. When she closed with, "I thank God that your dangers are over, while the glory of your deeds remains," there was a wild outburst of cheers. The men waved their hats, their sabers, anything and everything that would wave, and shouted till the hills echoed.

The sailors were no less loyal. During this same summer, there was a superb naval review off Spitshead which the Queen witnessed from the royal yacht. Two hundred and forty ships of war were assembled, but that was not all, for the Queen's suite alone consisted of thirty steamships, and there were many hundred private steamboats and sailing vessels. Every foot of the shore that would give a view of the warships was crowded with spectators, and they had a sight well worth the seeing. Ships and steamers were beautifully decorated with flags and crowded with guests. The men-of-war were drawn up in a double line, and the royal yacht steamed slowly along between them. Every vessel manned its yards and fired a royal salute as the Queen passed. The most enthusiastic cheering echoed and reechoed. Then came a mimic naval attack on Southsea Castle, and the brilliant day was at an end.

One thing more the Queen planned to do for her soldiers, and that was to give a badge of special honor to those who had been especially distinguished by some deed of rare bravery. This badge was the Victoria Cross, which was then bestowed for the first time. With it went a pension of fifty dollars a year. More than one hundred thousand people assembled in Hyde Park to see the sixty-two chosen heroes receive their Crosses. The Queen was now in the scarlet jacket of the army. Prince Albert rode on one side of her and Prince Frederick William on the other side. She remained on horseback during the whole ceremony, leaning forward as one brave fighter after another was led up to her, and pinning the Cross on his breast.

The woman whose battles had been, not with Russians, but with mismanagement and inefficiency, lingered in the Crimea until she had seen every soldier leave for home, then she herself returned as quietly as

NIS! NIS! NIS! HURRAH!

if she had been on a pleasure trip. She seemed to have entirely forgotten that thousands of men in England would have been lying in Crimean graves had it not been for her; but the men remembered, and England gave her such a welcome as even the Duke of Wellington had hardly received. She was an honored guest at Balmoral. Everyone was longing to do something for her, but what should it be?" "Make her a gift," said the people, "and let her do with it as she will." Two hundred and fifty thousand dollars was raised by popular subscription and presented to her. She did with it as she would; she endowed schools for the training of nurses to carry on the work that she loved.

CHAPTER X

THE ROYAL YOUNG PEOPLE

MANY people had thought that the Russians hoped to get control of India. If they had succeeded in doing so, the Queen would have been saved the sorrow that came to her from a revolt of her Indian troops which was known as the Sepoy Mutiny. The commanders of the troops were English, but most of the rank and file were either Mohammedans or Hindus. The Mohammedans looked upon the cow as sacred, and the Hindus regarded the hog as unclean, therefore, when cartridges were given them greased with a mixture of tallow and lard, the soldiers of both peoples were very angry. Another trouble was that the English government had declared that no one should lose his property on account of any change in his religious belief, and this decree aroused the wrath of the native priests. The revolt was one of the most fearful events known in history, for even women and children were murdered as brutally as if the Sepoys had been wild beasts.

January, 1858, was the time that had been set for the marriage of the Princess Royal, and although India was not entirely subdued, the Sepoys were so nearly under control that England could join heartily in the wedding rejoicings. Buckingham Palace was crowded with guests, so many princes and princesses that when they went to the theater, they made, as the Queen said, "a wonderful row of royalties." "Macbeth" and three other plays were performed in honor of the occasion. For a week, eighty or ninety persons sat at the Queen's dinner table every day. There were operas, dinner parties, dances, concerts, and a great ball at which one thousand guests were present.

When the wedding gifts began to arrive, the large drawing room of the palace became a veritable fairyland, as table after table was piled with presents. "Fritz," as the family called Prince Frederick William, had brought to his bride a necklace of pearls, which the Queen said were the largest she had ever seen. This was only the beginning. The Princess and her mother went for a little walk in the palace garden, and when they came in, there were more tables and an entirely new display of gifts; they went to their own rooms, and when they returned, still more gifts had arrived. There were pictures, candelabra, diamond and emerald bracelets, brooches, necklaces, everything in the shape of jewelry that can be imagined, and, what especially pleased the housewifely tastes of the Queen, there were quantities of needlework from many ladies of the kingdom, for the Princess was a special favorite, and rich and poor were eager to send her some token of their love. The young girl was in ecstasies; then she remembered that going with "Fritz" meant leaving her father and mother, and she burst into tears.

At the end of the festal week came the wedding day. The Queen said, "I felt as if I were being married over again myself, only much more nervous," and when just before the ceremony, she was daguerreotyped with "Fritz and Vicky," she trembled so that her likeness was badly blurred.

Early in the morning the bells began to ring, but long before their first peal, thousands were out in the streets, too excited to sleep or even to remain in their homes. The procession was formed just as it had been eighteen years before at the marriage of the Queen, and the long line of carriages drove from Buckingham Palace to the Chapel Royal of St. James. Trumpets were blown, banners were waved, and the whole city reëchoed with the shouts of the merrymakers. The Queen bowed to her people as graciously as ever, but she could not forget for a moment that her oldest daughter was about to leave her, and she wrote afterwards, "The cheering made my heart sick within me."

The procession was even more beautiful than that on the wedding day of the Queen, because in this one there were so many children. First came the members of the royal family, the Duchess of Kent nearest to the Queen and her children, looking very handsome in her gown of violet velvet trimmed with ermine. Then came the Prime Minister bearing the sword of state. He was followed by "Bertie," who was now a tall young man of sixteen, and "Affie," the sailor boy of fourteen, both in Highland costume. Everyone was looking for the Queen, and she came directly after her older sons. She was resplendent in a moiré skirt of lilac and silver with a long train of lilac velvet, and was all ablaze with diamonds. The two little boys, the namesake of the Duke of Wellington, and Leopold, who was not yet five, walked one on either side of their mother. They as well as the older boys were brilliant in Stuart plaid, which made a glowing contrast with the lilac velvet. Behind the Queen walked hand in hand the three royal girls, Alice who was fifteen, and the two younger ones, Helena and Louise. They were in pink satin with cornflowers and marguerites in their hair. The nine royal children were present, with the exception of baby Beatrice, who was not yet one year old. The Queen and the royal family took their places in the "Royal Closet," a room opening into the chapel.

All the guests had assembled long before the entrance of the procession, and now they were all watching eagerly for the Prince of Prussia and the Princess Royal of England. The Prince in his dark blue uniform, looked thoroughly a soldier. He made a profound bow to the Queen, knelt in prayer for a few minutes, then stood waiting to receive his bride. After the gorgeous colors worn by those who had preceded her, the white moiré dress and the wreath of orange blossoms and myrtle made the Princess look very childlike. She walked between her father and King Leopold, her train borne by the eight young girls who were her bridesmaids. They were in white tulle with pink roses. Among the roses were sprigs of white heather, for even in the excitement of this wedding season, the Queen did not forget her Scottish home.

The Prince was much more calm than the Archbishop of Canterbury, for the clergyman was so nervous that he left out some passages from the marriage service. At the moment that the ring was put on the finger of the bride, the cannon were fired as at the marriage of the Queen; but now the people of Germany must not be forgotten, and as the first gun sounded, a telegram was sent to Berlin. The last words of the service were read, "The Lord mercifully with his favor look upon you," and the "Hallelujah Chorus" burst forth, followed by Mendelssohn's "Wedding March," as the bride and bridegroom went forth from the chapel hand in hand.

All London was keeping holiday, and throngs had gathered about Buckingham Palace, ready to greet the returning party with most tumultuous applause. The honeymoon was to be spent at Windsor, and the Eton boys, who always claimed a share in royal rejoicings, dragged the royal carriage from the railroad station to the castle.

A few days later came the final good-bys, and these were much harder than if the bride had not been of the royal family, for kings and queens can make few visits. It was a very tearful time, "a dreadful day," wrote the Queen. "I think it will kill me to take leave of dear papa," the bride had said to her mother, but the moment of parting had to come. The snow was falling fast, but all the way to the wharf at Gravesend were beautiful decorations and crowds of people, and on the pier were companies of young girls wearing wreaths and carrying flowers to strew before the feet of the bride. "Come back to us if he doesn't treat you well," called a voice from the crowd, and the steamer moved slowly away from the wharf. Prince Albert watched it for a few minutes, then returned to the

Queen, who was lonely in her great palace, so lonely that even the sight of baby Beatrice made her sad, reminding her that only a few hours before the little one had been in the arms of the beloved eldest daughter.

"The little lady does her best to please him," Prince Albert had written on the day of the Princess's engagement; but now she had thousands of people to please, and the father and mother at home waited anxiously for letters and telegrams and reports of friends to know what welcome the Germans had given to their daughter, for so much of her future comfort among them depended upon the first impression that she made. "Dear child," wrote Prince Albert to, her, "I should have so liked to be in the crowd and hear what the multitude said of you." He had already received a proud and jubilant telegram from "Fritz,"—"The whole royal family is enchanted with my wife." The Princess Hohenlohe, the Queen's beloved half-sister, wrote from Berlin, "The enthusiasm and interest shown are beyond everything. Never was a princess in this country received as she is."

Later in the year, the royal father and mother contrived to make a fortnight's visit to Germany, and found the "Princess Frederick William" "quite the old Vicky still." Prince Albert's birthday was celebrated during their stay. The children at home were also celebrating it with the Duchess of Kent. They recited poems and played their pieces of music and exhibited the pictures that they had drawn. Several days earlier, they had all sent birthday letters to Germany, and these letters were given a prominent place on the "presents table." The Queen's gift to her husband was a portrait of baby Beatrice, done in oil. The Princess did not forget the Scotch home that she loved, and among her gifts to her father was an iron chair for the Balmoral garden.

The farewells had to be said much too soon. Then came the return to England and the other children. They were growing up fast. The Prince of Wales was at Oxford, not idling his time away, but working so hard that the irrepressible *Punch* called him "A Prince at High Pressure." Alfred, who was now fourteen, had just passed his examination and received his midshipman's appointment. The examiners would have been satisfied with fifty correct answers, but the Prince had presented eighty; and when his father and mother landed at Osborne, there he stood on the wharf in his naval cadet's uniform, half-blushing, and looking as happy as a boy who was not a prince would have looked after coming out of a three-days' examination with flying colors. Several months earlier, Prince Albert had watched him reef a topsail in a strong breeze, and said it almost took his breath away to see him "do all sorts of things at that dizzy height."

The circle of children soon began to widen, for early in 1859 Princess "Vicky" became the mother of a boy, and the Queen, not yet forty years of age, was a grandmother. The child was named Frederick William Victor Albert. Ever since her marriage, the Princess had kept up a constant correspondence with home. She wrote her mother every day, sometimes twice a day, telling all the little events of her life. To her father she sent every Monday long letters on general topics, and he always sent a reply two days later. No one knew better than he the difficulties that lay before her in making her home in a foreign country, and often his letters gave her bits of advice that had come from his own experience. Sometimes they were little pictures of home life. Once he told her of a "splendid snowman" that the children had made, with a yellow carrot for a nose and an old hat of "Affie's" on his head. After the birth of Frederick William Victor Albert, the letters from Germany never forgot to tell the latest news about the little German baby; and the English letters quoted the sayings of baby Beatrice, whom Prince Albert called "the most amusing baby we ever had." One day he wrote of this little one, "When she tumbles, she calls out in bewilderment, 'She don't like it, she don't like it.' She came into breakfast a short time ago with her eyes full of tears, moaning, 'Baby has been so naughty, poor baby so naughty,' as one might complain of being ill or of having slept badly."

While Buckingham Palace had still its merry group of children, the two older sons, "Bertie" and "Affie," were on their way across the ocean. Prince Alfred was making a voyage to the Cape of Good Hope, and the Prince of Wales was going to Canada. During the Crimean War, the colony had raised and equipped a regiment to aid the mother country, and had most urgently invited the monarch to visit her lands in the west; but because of the exposure and fatigue it was not thought wise for her to accept the invitation. Canada had then asked that one of the Princes should be appointed governor. They were far too young for any such position, but the promise was made that the Prince of Wales should visit the colony. In the spring of 1860 it was decided that he should go early in the autumn.

The Prince was delighted with the expedition, and was ready to be pleased with whatever came to hand. In Newfoundland a ball was given for him, and he danced not only with the ladies of the official circle, but with the wives and daughters of the fish-merchants, and had the tact to make himself liked by all. "He had a most dignified manner and bearing," said the wife of the Archdeacon. "God bless his pretty face and send him a good wife," cried the fishermen. His visit to Canada was not all amusement, for he had the usual royal duties to perform. He opened an exhibition, laid the last stone of the Victoria Bridge over the St. Lawrence, and laid the corner stone of the new parliamentary buildings at Ottawa. No fault could be found with his manner of attending to such duties, but he won the hearts of the people less by laying corner stones than by such bits of boyishness as singing with the band one day when they chanced to play some of his favorite airs. He saw Blondin walk across Niagara Falls on a tight-rope. "I beg of you, don't do that again," he said earnestly to the performer. "There is really not the least danger; I would willingly carry you over on my back," replied Blondin, but the Prince did not accept the offer.

When Mr. Buchanan, President of the United States, heard that the Prince of Wales was coming to Canada, he wrote to the Queen, inviting the Prince to visit him at the White House, and assuring her that her son would receive a very cordial greeting from the Americans. The city of New York meant to have a royal visit all to herself, and therefore sent a special invitation for him to come to that city. The United States showed no lack of interest in the young man. Reporters from the leading American papers followed him about in Canada; and when he crossed to Detroit, he found the whole city illuminated, and the streets so crowded that he had to slip into his hotel by the side entrance. He visited the grave of Washington, and planted a tree by the tomb of the man who had prevented him from becoming the ruler of all North America. His visit to the White House lasted for five days, and at its close, President Buchanan wrote to the Queen: "In our domestic circle he has won all hearts."

In New York a ball was given for him which he enjoyed; but he was far more enthusiastic over a parade of the New York Fire Department. Six thousand firemen in uniform turned out one evening, all with lighted torches except those who manned the ropes. A delightful trait in both his parents was their feeling that honors shown them were not merely actions due to their position, but were marks of courtesy and kindness; and the Prince showed this same characteristic, for at the review he cried with grateful delight, "It is splendid, and it's all for me, every bit for me!"

On the Prince's return voyage he was so delayed by contrary winds that two warships were sent out to search for him. He reached home late in November, and on his return a letter was written to President Buchanan by the Queen, expressing her gratitude for the kindness shown her son and speaking very warmly of the friendship between England and the United States.

IN THE DAYS OF QUEEN VICTORIA

While the Prince of Wales was receiving the honors of the western continent, the midshipman brother was on his way to South Africa. When he landed at Cape Town, the English governor accompanied him on a short tour through the English possessions, during which he laid the first stone of the famous breakwater in Table Bay. He was cheered and feasted and received with all the honors that could be devised so long as he was on land; but when he returned to his vessel, he was no longer treated as a prince; for on shipboard he was simply a midshipman and in no wise different from the other naval cadets. When the chief of an African tribe came to visit the ship, he saw the young Prince barefooted and helping the other midshipmen to wash the decks. The chief went away wondering, and a little later, he and his councilors sent to the English a most interesting letter. It read:

"When the son of England's great Queen becomes subject to a subject, that he may learn wisdom, when the sons of England's chiefs and nobles leave the homes and wealth of their fathers, and with their young Prince endure hardships and sufferings in order that they may be wise and become a defense to their country, when we behold these things, we see why the English are a great and mighty nation."

When the two brothers returned to England, they found that their sister Alice had followed the example of the Princess Royal and had become engaged. The fortunate man was Prince Louis of Hesse. Prince Albert wrote to his daughter in Germany of "the great

Alician event," saying, "Alice and Louis are as happy as mortals can be."

Not long after these cheerful times, a deep sorrow came to the loving heart of the Queen. In the midst of the days that were so full of care for her children, her home, and the duties of state not only in England, but also in Africa and Asia, the constant thought of the Queen had been her mother's comfort. When the daughter could not be with her mother, letters were sent every day, and frequently several times a day, and nothing was neglected that could add to the Duchess's ease and happiness. For some time she had not been well, and in the spring of 1861 came the dreaded summons to her bedside. In a few hours she was gone. "Oh, if only I could have been near her these last weeks!" wrote the Queen to King Leopold.

Save the sovereign herself, there was no woman in England whose death would have affected the whole country so deeply. Statesmen recalled the days when the Duchess of Kent was left alone in a strange land, without means, disliked by the reigning king, and weighed down by the responsibility of educating a child to stand at the head of the nation. In the character of their sovereign, they saw proof of the able, devoted, conscientious manner in which this sacred duty had been performed; and the address of sympathy sent by Parliament to the sorrowing Queen was as sincere as if it had been written by a personal friend, and not by a body of lawmakers. "It is a great sorrow to me not to have Féodore with me now," wrote the Queen to King Leopold; but neither he nor the Princess Hohenlohe was able to be present at the last services.

"I cannot imagine life without her," said the Queen sadly; but nevertheless, life had to go on. Others may sometimes stop to mourn, but the duties of a sovereign may not be neglected even for sorrow. A new cause of anxiety had arisen that came nearer home than even the sufferings of the Crimean soldiers. War had broken out in the United States, and the supply of cotton to England was rapidly diminishing. If the cotton supply failed entirely, the mills of England would have to stop; many thousands of spinners and weavers would have no work; and the sufferings of the manufacturing districts would be intense. The government made an earnest effort to increase the amount of cotton imported to England from India; but the emergency was so sudden that even during the first few months of the war, there were many honest, hardworking people in England who were sorely in need.

When autumn came, the Queen was free to go for a little while to the beloved Balmoral for the rest and quiet which she so greatly needed. The simple life of the Highlands did more for her than anything else could have done. On this visit, Prince Albert, the Queen, the Princess Alice, Prince Louis of Hesse, with Lady Churchill and General Grey in attendance, went on two of what the Queen called "Great Expeditions," that is, trips of two or three days by carriage and by pony. To the Queen these trips were as fascinating as they were novel. The party tried to keep their identity a secret, and sometimes they succeeded: Prince Albert and the Queen called themselves *Lord* and *Lady Churchill*; the real Lady Churchill was now *Miss Spencer*, and General Grey became *Dr. Grey*. They were as ex-

THE ROYAL YOUNG PEOPLE

cited as children in a new game over playing their parts properly, and the struggles of the two men-servants to remember not to say "Your Majesty" and "Your Royal Highness" amused them immensely. "The lady must be terrible rich," whispered an awestruck woman to one of the servants, "for she has so many gold rings on her fingers." "And you have many more than I," said the aggrieved monarch to Lady Churchill. Two or three times they stayed all night at little village inns. The Queen wrote in her journal that at one of them the bedroom given to her and the Prince was hardly more than large enough for the bed, but she found no fault with it, and called it "very clean and neat." The dinner was "nice, clean, and good" according to her description, for this sovereign of Great Britain, with several magnificent palaces of her own, was so ready to be pleased with what was done for her that she could be contented in the tiny inn of a Highland village. At a second inn, which seems to have been particularly poor, she admits that there was "hardly anything to eat," but closes her account less like the ruler of millions than like a half amused and half disappointed little schoolgirl, "No pudding and no fun. We soon retired."

The efforts to avoid being "found out" were like a continual frolic. The royal party trembled when they heard the distant sound of a drum and fife, but felt safe again on being told by a little maid at the inn that it was "just a band that walked about twice a week." Sometimes they came to tiny villages where they were "suspected;" and at last, on getting up one morning, they heard the tread of somewhat irregular marching, led by a drum and fife and bagpipe. There was no escape then, for they were found out at last. A company of volunteers was drawn up in front of the door to do them honor; the women of the village stood by with bunches of flowers in their hands; and the landlady was glorified by a black satin dress with white ribbons and orange blossoms. There was nothing to do but to bow with all gratitude and drive away as fast as possible.

Such a woman was Victoria of England, ready to be pleased with the smallest things, praising what was good, saying little of what was not good, and enjoying every little pleasure with a childlike zest and simplicity. And yet, this gentle little lady understood so perfectly her rights and duties as monarch of Great Britain that when her Secretary of Foreign Affairs persisted in being quite too independent in his methods of transacting business, she did not hesitate to write to him the following very definite sentences:

"The Queen thinks it right, in order to prevent any mistake for the future, to explain what it is she expects from the Foreign Secretary. She requires:

"1. That he will distinctly state what he proposes in a given case, in order that the Queen may know as distinctly to what she has given her royal sanction.

"2. Having once given her sanction to a measure, that it be not arbitrarily altered or modified by the Minister. She expects to be kept informed of what passes between him and the Foreign Ministers, before important decisions are taken, based upon that intercourse; to receive the foreign dispatches in good time, and to have the drafts for her approval sent to her in sufficient time to make herself acquainted with their contents before they must be sent off."

It is worth noting that the royal lady who wrote this epistle had sufficient self-control to delay for five months forwarding it to the offending Secretary, hoping that his methods would be amended and that so severe a rebuke would become unnecessary.

CHAPTER XI

THE QUEEN IN SORROW

IT had certainly become clear to all her Ministers that Victoria was no mere figurehead, for while she yielded if their judgment was against her, yet she never failed to have an opinion and a reason for her opinion. In 1861, the fact that both she and Prince Albert were able to think for themselves and had come to a wise conclusion proved to be a matter of the utmost importance to two countries, England and the United States. Everyone in England was thinking about the war in America. The English government had declared that England would be neutral, that is, it would do nothing to assist either the United States or the seceded States. The United States Government was indignant at this declaration, because it spoke of the seceded, or Confederate States, not as if they were rebelling against the government, but as if they were an independent power. The Confederate States, however, were much pleased, and thought it quite possible that England might be persuaded to help them. Their chief argument was—cotton. These States were the ones that raised cotton, and with the United States warships blockading their ports, there would be little chance for

THE QUEEN IN SORROW

cotton to reach England. Would not England, then, help the seceders, put an end to the war, and have all the cotton that her mills wished to use?

The Confederates decided to send two men, named Mason and Slidell, across the ocean for aid, the first to England, the second to France. It was not easy to get away from a southern port, but they contrived to escape to Havana, and from there they went on board a British mail steamer named the *Trent*. They supposed that all difficulties were over when they were once on board a British vessel; but before the *Trent* had been out twenty-four hours, a United States warship fired a shot across her bows. The *Trent* was not armed so that she could make any resistance, therefore she stopped, and Lieutenant Fairfax was sent aboard with a strong guard of marines.

"My orders from Captain Wilkes are to ask to see the list of your passengers," he said.

"That list cannot be shown," was the reply of the English captain.

"I am here to arrest Messrs. Mason and Slidell," Lieutenant Fairfax stated, but the Captain only bowed.

"It is well known to the United States authorities that they are attempting to make their way to Europe as envoys from States in rebellion against the government," said the Lieutenant, "and, therefore, I demand their surrender."

Then Commodore Williams, who was in charge of the mail, said indignantly:

"The two gentlemen are passengers in a British vessel which is carrying the mail from one neutral port to another. On board this ship I represent her Majesty's government. This thing is an outrage, and I tell you that you and your North shall suffer for it. Does your Captain Wilkes do this on his own responsibility or on that of your government?"

"On his own," was the reply.

"It is an insult to England and a violation of international law," declared the Commodore; but nevertheless the men were seized and carried to Boston.

When the news of this action reached England, there was wild excitement. Troops were sent to Canada at once. The Canadian harbors were frozen, and England had to ask permission of the United States to land them at Portland, Maine. Permission was granted, and no one seemed to see how amusing such a request was. Thousands of Englishmen were ready to declare war upon the United States without a moment's delay. Fortunately governments move more slowly than individuals, and war could not be declared without first asking whether the United States had given authority for the seizure or approved of it. Mr. Slidell's wife and daughter had gone on to England in the *Trent;* and they said Captain Wilkes did not claim to have any government authority, and that the United States would probably set the envoys free as soon as they reached Washington. The Prime Minister did not believe such would be the result, and he wrote a somewhat curt demand to the United States for an apology and the freedom of the two men.

THE QUEEN IN SORROW

Neither the Queen nor the Prince Consort, for that title had been granted to Prince Albert long before, was satisfied with this paper, and the following morning he wrote a statement to be sent to the Prime Minister to the effect that the paper ought to mention the friendship between the two countries and the hope and expectation of England that the United States would say the seizure was not done by government authority. Prince Albert and the Queen read the statement over together. She made two or three small changes in the wording, then copied it and sent it to the Prime Minister. He admitted at once that the Queen and the Prince were in the right, and wrote another dispatch to send to the United States, saying, of course, that an apology and the surrender of the men were expected, but wording the demand in a most courteous and friendly manner.

In the United States, as soon as President Lincoln heard of the capture, he said, "This won't do. Captain Wilkes is exercising the 'right of search,' and we fought England in 1812 on that very ground. Those men must be given up." There were thousands, however, who were so excited that they were ready to fight anybody for anything or for nothing, and if the Prime Minister's first dispatch had been sent, it would have been hard to prevent hostilities; but in so moderate a request for fairness, even the most hot-blooded could find little excuse for demanding a declaration of war.

So it was that Prince Albert and the Queen saved the two countries from bloodshed, and if the Prince had done nothing else in his twenty-one years of acting as chief adviser to the Queen, that one act would have been glory enough. But when one remembers the vast number of matters which he had to consider, it does not seem as if one man's mind could have held them all. Laying corner stones, unveiling statues, presiding over learned societies, guiding the education of his children, planning palaces, and managing large estates—all this was but a small part of his labors. He carried out reforms in the navy, he studied on commercial treaties between England and other countries, he reorganized the army, he wrote on improved methods of agriculture, he constructed better national defenses, he kept himself well informed concerning the condition of the United States, India, South Africa, and every country of Europe. After twenty-one years of such intense work as this, it is no wonder that he was exhausted. He rarely spoke of his weariness; but here and there in his letters and in his conversation with the Queen, a word was dropped that showed how weak and tired he felt. He slept little, yet he never thought of sparing himself, and he wrote the letter about the *Trent* affair with a very feeble hand. "I could hardly hold my pen while writing," he told the Queen, and at last he admitted that he was thoroughly miserable.

Then came day after day of illness. Sometimes the Prince would listen to his wife or his daughter Alice while they read him one of Scott's novels; once he asked for music a long way off, and a piano was brought into another room so that the Princess Alice could play his favorite *chorale*. Sometimes he was confused and recognized no one. "We are much alarmed," said the physicians, "but we do not give up hope."

THE QUEEN IN SORROW

Every day found him a little weaker, and soon the evening came when, as the Queen bent over him and whispered, "It is your own little wife," he could not speak, he could only bow his head and kiss her, and in a little while he was gone.

At midnight the mournful tolling of the great bell of St. Paul's spread the sorrowful news through the city of London, and the telegraph told the children of the royal family who were away from England of the loss that had befallen them.

The Princess Victoria was not alone, for her husband and her child were with her to give her comfort; but far away in the warm climate of Cannes was Prince Leopold, the delicate little boy of only eight years, with not one of his own family beside him. The child was already grieving sorely over the death of the gentleman in whose charge he had been when the telegraph brought the news of his crushing loss. "Oh, mamma, mamma," he cried. "Do take me to mamma. I want my mother. I want my mother."

The warmest sympathy was felt for the sorrowing Queen in her own land and in all lands. Even from some chiefs in New Zealand came an address, which began:

"Oh, Victoria, our mother, we greet you! All we can now do is to weep with you, oh, our good mother, who have nourished us, your ignorant children of this island, even to this day."

Every honor that could be shown was given to the dead Prince Consort. The Queen chose a sunny spot at Frogmore for the beautiful mausoleum that was to be built for the body of the one who had been dearest to her of all the world. Seven years earlier, she had said, "Trials we must have, but what are they, if we are together?" but now the time had come when she must bear alone whatever might befall her. Her greatest comforter was the Princess Alice, the girl of eighteen, who seemed no longer a merry young girl, but a sympathetic, self-controlled woman. She and the other children went with the Queen to Osborne, and there passed the first three months of the lonely woman's sorrow. King Leopold and the Princess of Hohenlohe came to her; but the weight of her grief was hers alone, and no one could lessen it.

Crushed as she was by suffering, she did not cease to feel for others. Within a month after the death of the Prince, a terrible colliery accident occurred by which many lives were lost, and the Queen sent at once a generous gift and the message, "Tell them that the Queen's own misery only makes her feel the more for them." In her own heartbreak she could not neglect the state business, whose delay would cause many difficulties, but she could not bear to meet others than her children and a few of her nearest friends. Again it was the Princes Alice upon whom she and the whole country relied, and this girl of eighteen went back and forth between the sovereign and the Ministers with such strength of mind, such thoughtfulness and tact, that the whole realm was amazed and grateful.

It would have been a comfort to the loving mother if she could have kept her oldest son with her during those months; but, even to lessen her loneliness, she would not break in upon the plans that his father had made for him. It had been decided that he should travel in the Holy Land, and not many weeks after the death of the Prince, he set out with Dean Stanley and others for the East.

It had long been the custom in the royal family to spend at Balmoral the Queen's birthday, in May, and the birthday of the Prince, in August, and even during this sad year of 1862, the usual May visit was made. Hard as it was for the Queen to go without the Prince to a place that had been so dear to him, there was comfort for her in going among the cottagers. She loved the Scotch because, while they had a profound respect for her, they had also, respect for themselves, and would talk with her without the subservience that she disliked. She taught her Scotch tenants to look upon her as a friend to whom they might come for help in time of trouble. In sickness they were encouraged to send to the castle for whatever they needed. When the Queen went to London, she did not forget them, and whenever a marriage or a death or the arrival of a new baby occurred among her Balmoral people, it was reported to her at once.

During the last visit of the Prince Consort to Balmoral, the husband of one of the cottagers was very ill, and the Queen was continually sending him delicacies from her own table, and not always by the hands of servants, for the Princess Louise was often her messenger. The story is told of the young girl's taking some dainty from one of the pockets of her jacket and asking, "Can't he eat this?" and then, when the wife shook her head sadly, of her taking something else from another pocket and saying, "Surely, he can eat this." The husband died, and when the Queen arrived at Balmoral on this first visit without the Prince, she went at once to see the widow. Both women burst into tears.

"I ask your pardon," said the cottager humbly. "I ought not to cry in your presence."

"Oh, it does me good," replied the Queen in the midst of her own tears. "I am so thankful to cry with someone who knows just how I feel. It was all so sudden, so sudden."

This visit to Balmoral was in May, and in July the brave-hearted Queen gave away her chief comforter, for she did not think it right to allow the marriage of the Princess Alice to be postponed longer. Many preparations for it had already been made before the illness of the Prince. The Highlanders were all interested in the marriage, for the Princess Alice was a great favorite among them; and in the autumn of 1861, many wedding gifts had been made by the Princess to the cottagers, for in the Queen's family it was the custom to make presents as well as receive them at the wedding seasons.

The marriage took place at Osborne. The day which all had expected to be so bright and happy was sad and lonely for the want of the dead Prince. There was no rejoicing, for everything was so associated with him that no one could be merry. Even the wedding dress of the bride was of lace, whose pattern he himself had chosen.

THE QUEEN IN SORROW

In a few days Prince Louis and the Princess Alice left England for their German home. According to what had become a custom among the Queen's children, the Princess wrote to her mother almost every day. Her life in Darmstadt was far more simple than the Queen's had been immediately after her marriage. The usual time of rising was half-past seven or a little earlier. Coffee was drunk at eight, and generally the next two hours were spent out of doors in riding or walking. From ten to twelve, the Princess wrote or worked with her private secretary, and some time in the morning she read the newspapers, an occupation which she called "a great bore." Breakfast took the time between twelve and one. At two, people began to come to call upon her. Dinner was at four. After dinner came a little leisure, then a drive "some where for tea." By half-past ten the day was over. The Princess lamented that she had so little time for her music and drawing, and when she was away from the city, she made many sketches, but she was in a wooded country, "And the trees are my misfortune," she said, "as I draw them so badly." After a few months, the twelve-year-old brother Arthur went to visit her. He was a bit of home, and she was delighted to have him. "He has won all hearts," she wrote to the Queen, "and I am so proud when they admire my little brother." When September came, the Princess and her husband went to Thuringia to meet the Queen; and there, much to the Queen's pleasure, it was decided that her daughter and Prince Louis should spend the winter in England, though the Princess with her ready sympathy wrote that she should regret not remaining in Germany for the one reason that the people would feel her absence so much. "They are most kind," she added, for she shared the feeling of her mother that the devotion of the people was not a thing that they could demand, but was a personal kindness shown to them.

On this visit to the Continent, Queen Victoria spent a few days in Belgium with King Leopold; and while she was with him, a young girl was invited to be his guest whom she was especially desirous of meeting. Her name was Alexandra, and she was the eldest daughter of the heir to the throne of Denmark. She had grown up in the quaint old palace in Copenhagen within hearing of the murmur of the sea. When summer came, she was taken to a delightful house in the woods, where she had dogs and ponies and flowers and long walks through the forest; and when friends came from the town, there were picnics and boating and all sorts of good times. Indeed, every day was a kind of picnic, for in the country home the family almost lived out of doors, and there were always her two brothers and three sisters for company.

The life of the children was merry and happy, but it was even more simple than that of the little girl who went from Kensington to the throne of England, both because the father and mother believed that it was best for children to live simply, and also because, especially during the children's earlier years, there was not much money to throw away in luxuries. The little girls put on their nicer dresses, which perhaps their mother had made, when they were going out; but as soon as they came back and were ready to play, the street dresses were exchanged for something more substantial. The children had learned when they were

THE QUEEN IN SORROW

very young that they could not have everything they wanted and that they must be obedient and helpful and punctual. If they were not ready for a meal or for their lessons, they were often sent to their rooms as a punishment. Those rooms had to be in perfect order, for each daughter was required to take care of her own. As they grew older, they were taught to do many things for themselves. If one of them wanted a new dress and her rather slender allowance would not pay the dressmaker, she knew how to make it for herself; and if a new hat was wanted, she could trim it.

This was the way in which the young girl had grown up who was going to visit the Queen of Great Britain when her first year of sorrow was drawing to its close. This was no ordinary visit, for several persons were very anxious that the Queen should like the Princess. They need not have feared. Everyone who met Alexandra loved her, for this bright, cheerful young girl carried sunshine wherever she went, and it shone upon even the lonely heart of the sorrowful Queen.

There had been a great deal of discussion about who would be the bride of the Prince of Wales, and not a little scheming among no lesser people than some of the great dignitaries of Europe; for there were several young princesses whose parents would have been glad to form an alliance with the heir of England's crown. But while the schemers were scheming, the Prince was forming a very definite opinion of his own. At the home of his grandaunt, the Duchess of Cambridge, he saw one day a portrait of a very beautiful young girl.

"And who is that?" he asked his cousin, the Princess Mary.

"That's Alix," was the reply, "and she is the dearest girl in all the world. You know that grandfather left his palace of Rumpenheim to his six children and asked them to meet there every two years. We all go, and now there are twenty or more of us cousins, but Alix is the prettiest and sweetest and dearest of us all. You must have seen her, for she came to visit me when she was ten years old, and she went to a children's party at Buckingham Palace."

Boys of twelve do not always remember little girls of ten. The Prince of Wales did not say whether he had forgotten "Alix" or not, but while, in 1861, the officials were talking about several other European princesses as well as the Princess Alexandra, he was making it clear to his father and mother that *she* was the one whom he wished to see. Princess "Vicky" always had her own opinions, and she too had been charmed by the lovely Danish Princess. "Come and visit me, and you shall see her," she wrote. The Prince went to Germany, the Princess was on her way to Rumpenheim, and nothing was easier than to arrange a meeting. Prince Albert wrote, "The young people seem to have a warm liking for each other." Some months after the death of Prince Albert, the two met again; next followed the little visit to Queen Victoria, and the loving welcome to the young girl who then became the betrothed of the Prince of Wales.

Denmark was delighted, and England was no less happy. Prince Christian soon carried his daughter to London to visit Queen Victoria; and then came a busy time, for all the wedding trousseau except the lingerie was to come from England. Princess Mary was delighted to help in selecting, and probably the Prince of Wales had now and then a word to say. While this was going on in England, scores of women in Denmark were cutting and stitching the finest of linen and embroidering on every article a crown and the initials of their beloved Princess. The whole land subscribed to give her a generous dowry, and then the wedding presents began to come. There were many of great value, of course, for all the courts of Europe were interested in the marriage; but the Princess cared most for the gifts that came from her own people, who knew her and loved her. Among those tokens there was a painting of her brothers and sisters in a group, a pair of shoes embroidered in gold from the shoemakers of Copenhagen, and some vases from the villagers who lived near the summer home in the forest. The Danish king gave her a necklace of diamonds and pearls, and King Leopold sent her a most beautiful dress of Brussels lace. At the end of the last sermon that she heard in her own church, the pastor, who had known her from babyhood, gave her a loving benediction and farewell.

The wedding was to be in England, and in February of 1863 the young bride with her father and mother and brothers and sisters went aboard the royal train. The Queen had sent to Antwerp her own *Victoria and Albert*, the yacht that had so often carried happy people, and after a few days' rest at King Leopold's court, the party crossed the Channel with a little squadron of British men-of-war as escort. As they neared the English coast, the water swarmed with every kind of vessel that would float, from a steamship to a rowboat, for everyone was eager to see the young girl whose beauty had been heralded throughout the kingdom. There was one boat which had the right of way, and soon the Prince of Wales was meeting his bride and giving her a hearty, old-fashioned kiss that satisfied even the hundreds of spectators. Her dress would seem to-day exceedingly quaint, but it must have been wonderfully becoming. It was of mauve poplin, made very full, for those were the days of hoop-skirts. Over it she wore a long purple velvet cloak with a border of sable, and her lovely face was framed in a white "poke" bonnet trimmed with rose-buds.

As soon as she had landed the difficulties began; for the people who had been waiting for hours to see the face that they had heard was the prettiest in the world meant to see it, and they thronged about her carriage in such determined crowds that the police were helpless. There is a story that one inquisitive youth actually twisted his head between the spokes of her carriage wheels to get a glimpse of her in some way; and the legend says that the Princess herself helped him out of his dangerous position. Addresses were presented before she had fairly set her feet upon English soil, one of them signed by the eight hundred Eton boys. Whenever there was a moment's delay, some delegation was always waiting, ready to make a speech of welcome. There were rockets and bonfires and salutes from vessels and forts, and, fascinated as she was, the young girl was thoroughly tired before she was safe at Windsor Castle.

A week later the royal wedding was celebrated in St. George's Chapel. The Prince was in the long flowing purple velvet mantle of the Order of the Garter, which made a rich contrast with the white lace and satin and orange blossoms of his bride. She was loaded with jewels, for the gifts of the Queen, the Prince, and the city of London must all be treated with respect. In her bouquet were sprigs of myrtle that had a history, for they had come from a bush grown from the myrtle in the bridal bouquet of the Princess "Vicky." There was more jewelry that was of special interest, for while the Prince was satisfied with a plain hoop of gold for the wedding ring, the guard was set with stones the initials of whose names formed the word, "Bertie,"—beryl, emerald, ruby, turquoise, jacinth, emerald. The lockets that he gave to the bridesmaids were made after a new fashion, for they were wrought of crystal, and in each were the initials "A. E.—A." intertwined in a design drawn by the Princess Alice. These letters were made of diamonds and coral to display the red and white of the Danish flag.

There was all the brilliancy and gorgeousness that can be imagined, for it was the wedding of the heir to the British crown. There were heralds, drummers, and trumpeters, all in quaint and handsome costumes. The gleam of gold, the flash of diamonds, and the burning glow of rubies made the Chapel a wilderness of color and brightness. Very slowly the beautiful Princess and her bridesmaids moved up the long aisle to the altar, too slowly for the comfort of Prince Arthur and his brother Leopold in their Highland dress, for the small German nephew had been put under their care, and the naughty little Frederick William Victor Albert bit their bare legs whenever they told him to be quiet.

The whole floor of the Chapel was radiant with beauty and aglow with happiness, but in the "Closet," up above the heads of the joyous throng, stood the Queen of England in the deepest mourning, glad in the gladness of her eldest son and in her love for the maiden who was his choice, but with the sorrow at her heart that forbade her to share in the rejoicings of her people.

CHAPTER XII

THE LITTLE FOLK

IN the midst of all the royalties that were present at the wedding of the Prince of Wales were the two great novelists of the realm, Thackeray and Dickens; but Tennyson, the Poet Laureate, was not there. Again "someone had blundered," and his invitation had been missent. Both the Queen and Prince Albert felt a sincere admiration and reverence for the poet, and the Prince had asked the favor of an autograph with far more hesitation than most schoolboys would have shown. This is the way in which he made his very modest petition:

"Will you forgive me if I intrude upon your leisure with a request which I have thought some little time of making, viz., that you would be good enough to write your name in the accompanying volume of the 'Idylls of the King'?" Prince Albert was very fond of the "Idylls," and when, only a month after his death, Tennyson brought out a new edition of the poems, it contained a beautiful dedication, which began:

"These to his memory—since he held them dear."

IN THE DAYS OF QUEEN VICTORIA

The lines do not sound as if the poet felt obliged to write them because he had been appointed Laureate, but rather as if he meant every word that he wrote. In this dedication he speaks very earnestly of Prince Albert's wisdom and ability and unselfishness, and gives us the exquisite line which everyone quotes who writes of the Prince Consort:

"Wearing the white flower of a blameless life."

The following year, just before the wedding of the Prince of Wales, Tennyson wrote a welcome to the bride, beginning:

"Sea-kings' daughter from over the sea, Alexandra!
Saxon and Norman and Dane are we,
But all of us Danes in our welcome of thee, Alexandra!"

The Queen was much pleased with the poem and said, "Thank him very warmly, and tell him with how much pleasure I have read the lines, and that I rejoice the sweet and charming bride should be thus greeted."

There is a story that when the Danish Princess was a very young girl, she and three of her girl friends sat together in the forest talking of what they should like to do when they were grown up.

"I want to be famous," said one. "I want to paint a picture that everyone will go to see, or to write a book that all Denmark will be eager to read."

THE LITTLE FOLK

"If I could do just what I liked," declared the second, "I would travel all over the world; so I will wish to be a great traveler."

"I want to be rich," said the third, "and then I can travel whenever I choose, and buy all the books I choose without having to write them, and all the pictures I choose without having to paint them. But what do you want, Alix?"

The Princess Alix had been thinking, and she answered slowly, "If I could have just what I wanted, I would choose that everyone who saw me should love me."

However it was with the others, the Princess Alexandra surely had her wish, for everyone who met her seemed to love her. The Queen called her "the fairy," and so great a dignitary as Dean Stanley thought of her in the same way, for after he had had a long talk with her in the corner of the drawing room, telling her how the service of the Church of England differed from that of the Danish Church, he wrote in his diary, "She is as charming and beautiful a creature as ever passed through a fairy tale." "The little gem of Denmark is the pet of the country," declared the newspapers. The unbounded admiration that had been shown to Queen Victoria in the early days of her reign was given to Alexandra. When the Queen came to the throne, young girls who were small and had fair hair and blue eyes were happy. *Now*, it was bliss to have any feature that resembled the Danish Princess. She had a custom of letting two curls of brown hair fall on each shoulder, and straightway English fashions demanded that every girl should wear four curls hanging on her shoulders. For months London was at the height of gayety. The Princess represented her royal mother-in-law at the drawing rooms of the season; no easy task, for so many ladies attended the first that it took four long hours for them to pass the throne. All this time the Princess Alexandra and the Princess Alice stood to receive them, except for one little resting time of twenty minutes. There were receptions and most magnificent balls, at which all the dignitaries tried their best to make themselves agreeable to the young Princess.

Of course the Queen had no heart for these festivities, but she was glad to have the people pleased, and for one of the most elaborate entertainments she sent decorations and furnishings from Buckingham Palace. The Princess Alice and Prince Louis were with her for several months before the marriage of the Prince of Wales; and only three or four weeks after the great event, a little Hessian granddaughter was born at Windsor Castle. The chaplain of the Hessian court came to England for the christening of the wee maiden. The usual number of names was given her, but the first two were Victoria Alberta.

In the autumn the Queen made the customary visit to Balmoral; but only a few days after her arrival she took an evening drive that put her into a great deal of danger, for the carriage turned over, and the Queen, the Princess Alice, and "Lenchen," as the Princess Helena was called, were thrown out. Brown, the Queen's favorite Highland attendant, had little regard for court manners at any time, and less than ever in this predicament. He called out, "The Lord Almighty have mercy on us! Who did ever see the like of this before! I thought you were all killed." The Queen had fallen on her face, and was somewhat bruised. Princess Alice, with her usual calmness, held a lantern so that the men could see to cut the horses free. Then while the driver went for help, the monarch of Great Britain sat in the road wrapped up in plaids and using the floor of the carriage for a back. The Princess had brought her page along, a Malay boy whose father had presented him to a traveler in return for some kindness, and little "Willem" sat in front with one lantern, while Brown held another. It was a strange situation, a Queen, with thousands of soldiers at her command, sitting in a broken carriage waiting for horses and guarded by one Highlander and a little black boy. She wrote in her journal for that day: "People were foolishly alarmed when we got upstairs, and made a great fuss. Had my head bandaged and got to bed rather late."

This soldier's daughter could make little of pain, but she could not so easily put away sorrow. Every place about Balmoral reminded her of something that Prince Albert had said or done, and she could not bear that his presence should be forgotten. On the summit of a hill which they had often visited together, she built a great cairn, on which was inscribed, "To the beloved memory of Albert, the great and good Prince Consort; raised by his broken-hearted widow, Victoria R."

She was touched and grateful when the citizens of Aberdeen wished to put up a statue of the Prince, and asked her to be present at the unveiling. It was nearly two years since his death, but she had not yet taken part in any public ceremony, and she dreaded to have the morning come. When it did come, however, she wrote in her journal the words that were the keynote of her courage in meeting difficulties, "Prayed for help and got up earlier." The rain poured, but the streets of Aberdeen were thronged with people. Out of sympathy with her grief, there was no cheering, and no band playing. For more than twenty-five years she had never appeared on public occasions without both cheering and music; and although she appreciated the thoughtful sympathy of the people, the silence only made the contrast greater between the past and the present. The exercises began with an address to the Queen by the Lord Provost. She handed him a written reply. Then he knelt before her; her Minister gave her a sword; and touching the Provost with it on each shoulder, she said "Rise, Sir Alexander Anderson." Mr. Anderson had now become a knight, and would be called Sir Alexander all the rest of his life. After this little ceremony, the bunting was drawn away from the statue, and what the Queen called a "fearful ordeal" was at an end.

The one upon whom the Queen depended most was Princess Alice. She often went on little picnics or drives "because Alice advised." The Princess and Prince Louis spent as much time in England as possible, and when they were in Germany the letters of the Princess gave her mother a great deal of pleasure. They were full of the details of her daily life, some of which might have come from a palace and some from a cottage. One described a gift just received from the Empress of Russia, "a splendid bracelet;" and a few days later, the young mother wrote exultantly that the baby

THE LITTLE FOLK

looked about and laughed. This young housekeeper was deeply interested in all the details of her home. She was grateful to her Queen mother for the big turkey pie and the other good things that arrived at Christmas time; and she wrote of her various little dilemmas, ranging all the way from a half-hour's hunt for a pen just after a journey to the whirl of making the dining room into a bedroom to accommodate a guest. One morning she wrote "in the midst of household troubles," as she said, for the Emperor and Empress had just sent word that they were coming to breakfast with her, and "Louis" was out. But of all the bits of home life in her letters, those about the children—for in a year and a half there was also a little Elizabeth—must have given the most pleasure to the royal Grandmamma. On one page the Princess described some political complication between kingdoms, and on the next was the astounding news that little Victoria could get on her feet by the help of a chair and could push it across the room. Before long, she was walking out with her father before breakfast, with her independent little hands in her jacket pockets. Money was not especially plenty in the home at Darmstadt, and the Princess mother wrote at one time of the little Elizabeth's wearing Victoria's last year's gowns, and at another said that she had just made seven little dresses for the children. With a German father and an English mother, the little Victoria spoke at first a comical combination of German and English, and she announced one day, "Meine Grossmama, die Königin, has got a little vatch with a birdie."

There was also a little boy in England who was taking much of the Queen's attention, the baby son of the Prince of Wales. He was born at Frogmore House, and as all the clothes provided for him were at Marlborough, he fared no better for raiment at first than if he had been born in a cottage. The loss was made up to him, however, when he was christened; for then he was gorgeous in a robe of Honiton lace, the same one in which his father had been christened, while over the robe was a cloak of crimson velvet with a lining of ermine. Nothing could be too rich and costly, for some day, if he lived long enough, he would wear the English crown. One matter in which the royal family were most economical was in regard to names, for they used the same ones over and over. This little boy was named Albert, for his English grandfather; Victor, for the Queen; Christian, for his Danish grandfather; and Edward, for his father. Princess "Alix" was as eager to be with her precious baby as the Queen had been to stay with her children, and she looked like a mischievous child when she had succeeded in slipping away from some grand company long enough to give baby "Eddie" his bath and put him to bed.

The little Princess Beatrice was scarcely more than a baby herself, but she seems to have felt all the responsibility of being aunt to so many small people. When she was hardly more than three years old, Princess "Vicky's" second child was born, and then Prince Albert wrote of the little girl to his eldest daughter, "That excellent lady has now not a moment to spare. 'I have no time,' she says when she is asked for anything. 'I must write letters to my niece!' "

THE LITTLE FOLK

Around her and across the Channel were children in whom she was most warmly interested, but the Queen's own childhood was rapidly growing more distant, not only by the passing of time, but also by the death of those who were most closely associated with her early days. Bishop Davys died in 1864, and in 1865 the death of King Leopold occurred. He was well called "the wisest king in Europe," and more than one dispute between kingdoms had been left to him for settlement. He knew all the royal secrets, and he made a judicious and kindly use of his knowledge. Ever since the Queen's accession he had aided her with his counsel, and now there was no one to whom she could look for disinterested advice. In that same year the assassination of President Lincoln occurred. The Queen was not satisfied with a formal telegram of regret; she wrote a letter, not as the sovereign of England to the wife of the President, but as one sorrowing woman to another, expressing her warm sympathy.

Few people realized how much severe mental labor the Queen had to endure. Often in the course of a single year many thousand papers were presented to her, and of these there were few to which she did not have to give close thought. For twenty-one years she had discussed everything with Prince Albert, and when they had come to a conclusion, he would, as in the *Trent* affair, write whatever was necessary. Then they would read the paper together and make any changes that seemed best. After his death, the Queen had to do all this work alone. She could wear the Kohinoor diamond, and she could build a million-dollar palace if she chose, but there were few persons in the kingdom

IN THE DAYS OF QUEEN VICTORIA

who worked harder than she. What belonged strictly to matters of state was more than enough for one person, but besides this there were schools, hospitals, and bazaars to open, prizes to distribute and corner stones to lay. Then there were entertainments, fêtes, receptions, balls, etc., frequently in behalf of some good object, whose success was sure if it could be said that the Queen would be present. The Prince and Princess of Wales could not lessen the weight of the public business that pressed so heavily upon the Queen, but they could relieve her from the strain of these public appearances, and this they did. They were both beloved by the people, but after the Queen had lived for five years in retirement, some of her subjects began to complain.

"What has she to do," grumbled one, "but to wear handsome clothes, live in a palace, and bow to people when she drives out?"

"Yes," declared another, "she has nothing to do. Parliament makes the laws, and she just writes her name."

"She's good to her cottagers in the Highlands," said a Londoner, "but she ought to care a little for the merchants here in London. Everybody likes the Princess, but the Queen's the Queen, and there never were such sales as when she was giving her fancy-dress balls."

"She thinks of nothing but her own sorrow," said another. "She has lost all sympathy with the people."

THE LITTLE FOLK

This last speech was made at a public meeting. Mr. John Bright, the "great peace statesman," was present, and he replied to it. His closing words were, "A woman who can keep alive in her heart a great sorrow for the lost object of her life and affection is not at all likely to be wanting in a great and generous sympathy for you."

Little by little the Queen learned the feelings of her people, and she soon published a response which must have made the grumblers feel ashamed. She said she was grateful for their wish to see her, but so much was now thrown upon her which no one else could do that she was overwhelmed with care and anxiety, and did not dare to undertake "mere representation," lest she should become unable to fulfill the duties which were of real importance to the nation. Some months later, she wrote of herself in a private letter: "From the hour she gets out of bed till she gets into it again, there is work, work, work—letter-boxes, questions, etc., which are dreadfully exhausting."

The Queen wished sincerely not only to do what was best for the people, but also to please them. She could not go to balls and theaters, but early in 1866 she determined to open Parliament in person. The London world rejoiced. They tried to imagine that the old days had come again, and they put on their jewels and their most splendid robes. All the way to the Parliament Building the streets were full of crowds who shouted "Long live the Queen! Hurrah for the Queen!" In the House of Lords there was a most brilliant assembly. Silks rustled and jewels sparkled as all rose to welcome the sovereign. As she entered, the

Prince of Wales stepped forward and led her to the throne. The royal Parliamentary robes with all their glitter of gold and glow of crimson were laid upon it, for the Queen wore only mourning hues, of deep purple velvet, trimmed with white miniver. On her head was a Marie Stuart cap of white lace, with a white gauze veil flowing behind. The blue ribbon of the Garter was crossed over her breast, and around her neck was a collar of diamonds. All the radiant look of happiness with which those were familiar who had seen her on the throne before, was gone. She was quiet and self-controlled, but grave and sad. Instead of reading her speech, she gave it to the Lord Chamberlain. At its close, she stepped down from the throne, kissed the Prince of Wales, and walked slowly from the room.

The Queen's two daughters, Helena and Louise, had attended her in opening Parliament. This must have been a little embarrassing for the older one, inasmuch as the Queen's address declared that the royal permission had been given for the Princess Helena to marry Prince Christian of Schleswig-Holstein; but members of the royal family cannot always consult their own feelings. When they rule different countries, it is not always easy for them even to remain friendly. The fact that the Queen, her daughters, and her Danish daughter-in-law were as fond of one another at the end of 1866 as they were at the beginning of 1864 is proof that the English royal family were very harmonious. Trouble had arisen between Denmark and the German states in regard to the duchies of Schleswig-Holstein, and in 1864 war had broken out between the little kingdom of Denmark and the united powers of

THE LITTLE FOLK

Prussia and Austria. Both countries were anxious to win the help of England. Princess "Vicky" and Princess Alice naturally sympathized with the German states; while Princess Alexandra's affection was of course with her own home land, which had now become her father's kingdom. The Emperor of France did not wish to have the German states increase in power, and he was ready to help Denmark, provided England would stand by him. England was willing, but England's sovereign would not hear to any talk of war with Germany, and the Ministers hesitated to act against her decided opposition. Of course the Danish Princess was grieved that the Queen would not consent to help her beloved country. Bismarck was the German statesman who was pushing on the war, therefore he was the man who was most abhorrent to the Princess of Wales. There is a story that the Queen had promised the little Beatrice a present, and that when she asked, "What shall it be?" the wee maiden, who had been carefully tutored by her sister-in-law, replied demurely, "Please, mamma, I'd like the head of Bismarck on a charger."

Two years later, there was a still more difficult condition of affairs in the Queen's family, for now that Prussia and Austria held the Schleswig-Holstein duchies, it was a question to which of the two powers they should belong; and to complicate matters even more, Princess Helena had married Prince Christian. Prussia and the north German states held together, and Austria joined the forces of the south German states. Prince "Fritz" belonged to the north and Prince Louis to the south, and therefore the husbands of the two

English Princesses were obliged to fight on opposite sides. The war lasted for only seven weeks, but it was an anxious time for Queen Victoria, who shared so fully in the troubles of her daughters. Princess Alice's two little girls were sent to England to be safe in her care, but in the midst of the war, a third little daughter was born. The boom of the distant guns was heard as she lay in her cradle in Darmstadt. Wounded men were being brought into the town, and the residents were fleeing in all directions. By and by the end came, and then the little dark-eyed baby was named Irene, or peace. Never before had a child so many godfathers, for when Prince Louis said farewell to his cavalry, he delighted them by asking the two regiments, officers and men, to be sponsors to his little girl.

CHAPTER XIII

MOTHER AND EMPRESS

WHILE the German wars were going on the Queen was thinking for her country as a sovereign and feeling for her children as a mother. In the midst of all the claims upon her, she had one aim that she never forgot, and that was to make her country understand and appreciate the talents and character of Prince Albert. She concluded to have a book prepared that should tell the story of his life, for she felt that no one who really knew him could fail to honor him. When the first volume was published, even her children were surprised that she should tell matters of her own private life so fully; but she loved and trusted her people, and she was as frank with them as she would have been with an intimate friend.

The year after this book was brought out, the Queen herself became the author of a book, "Our Life in the Highlands." It is made up of extracts from the journal which she always kept. "Simple records," she calls them, but they often give charming pictures of the merry times at Balmoral. Sir Arthur Helps aided her in preparing the book for the press. "He often scolds me," she said, "because I am careless in writing; but how could he expect me to take pains when I wrote late at night, suffering from headache and exhaustion, and in dreadful haste?" She arranged to have Sir Theodore Martin complete the life of the Prince, and she spent much time in arranging her husband's papers and letters for him to use. She generally chose the selections to be inserted, and she read every chapter as it was written.

About her own authorship the Queen was very modest, and when she sent a copy of her book to Dickens, she wrote in it, "From the humblest of writers to one of the greatest." At Sir Walter Scott's home, she was asked to write her name in his journal; and, although she granted the request, she wrote in her own journal, "I felt it a presumption in me." When Carlyle met her, he said, "It is impossible to imagine a politer little woman; nothing the least imperious, all gentle, all sincere; makes you feel too (if you have any sense in you) that she is Queen."

Her being Queen gave her a peculiar power over the marriages of her children, for they were not legal unless she gave her formal consent. Early in 1871 she was called upon again to exercise her right, for far up in the hills about Balmoral there was a momentous little interview between the Princess Louise and the Marquis of Lorne. "Princess Louise is so bright and jolly to talk with," one of the Scotch boys had said of her when she was a very young girl, and this Scotch Marquis was of exactly the same opinion.

MOTHER AND EMPRESS

The Queen had guessed before how matters stood with her daughter and the gentleman whom she had once called "such a merry, independent child." The young man had proved his independence by asking for the hand of the Princess, inasmuch as it was three hundred years since a member of the royal family had married a subject, but the Queen paid no attention to tradition. She felt sure that the Marquis would make her daughter happy, and that was enough. Most of her subjects agreed with her; and one of the newspapers said jubilantly, "The old dragon Tradition was routed by a young sorcerer called Love."

The wedding was celebrated at Windsor. It was a brilliant scene, of course, and if all the gentlemen were arrayed as vividly as the Duke of Argyll, the father of the bridegroom, the ladies did not monopolize gorgeousness of attire. The Duke was a Scottish chieftain, and he appeared in Highland dress. His kilt and the plaid thrown over his shoulders were of the gay Campbell tartan. His claymore, a broad two-handed sword, was at his side, and in front there hung from his belt a sporran, or deep pouch made of skin with the hair or fur on the outside. His dirk sparkled with jewels. Altogether he might have stepped out of some resplendent assemblage of the middle ages. After the wedding breakfast, the bride laid aside her white satin and Honiton lace and arrayed herself in a traveling dress of Campbell plaid. The carriage door was closed, and the young couple drove away for Claremont in a little shower of white slippers, accompanied, according to Highland tradition, by a new broom, which was sure to bring happiness to the new household.

IN THE DAYS OF QUEEN VICTORIA

The Queen's daughters were now in homes of their own except the Princess Beatrice, a merry little girl of fourteen, who had been radiantly happy in her new pink satin at her sister's wedding. The Queen was devoted to her children, but it would have been easier for her to pass through the next few years if she had been all sovereign and not woman. War broke out between France and Germany, and both Prince "Fritz" and Prince Louis were in the field. Anxious as she was for them, she was even more troubled for the Princess Alice, who was really in quite as much danger as if she had been in the army. For several years she had been deeply interested in lessening the sufferings of the poor in times of illness; and in providing trained nurses for wounded soldiers. While this war was in progress, she not only went to the hospitals daily, but she brought the wounded men to her own house and cared for them herself. She was exposed over and over again to typhus fever and other diseases, but she seemed to be entirely without fear. One of her friends describes seeing her help to lift a soldier who was very ill of smallpox.

Princess Alice little thought of what value her skill in nursing would be to her own family, but near the end of 1871, the Prince of Wales was taken ill with typhoid fever, and her help was of the utmost value. It was just ten years before that Prince Albert had died of the same disease, and to the anxious Queen every day was an anniversary. She hastened to the home of the Prince at Sandringham, and when she saw how ill he was, she sent at once for the other members of the family. The days passed slowly. One day he seemed a little better, and there was rejoicing, as the telegraph flashed the news not only over England, but to Canada, India, to every part of the world. Then came a day of hopelessness. The Queen mother watched every symptom. "Can you not save him?" she pleaded; and all the physicians could answer was, "You must be prepared for the worst. We fear that the end is near."

Bulletins were sent out to the public every hour or two. All London seemed to tremble with fear and anxiety. Stores were open, but there was little of either buying or selling. Day and night the citizens crowded the streets in front of the newspaper offices. They talked of no one but the Prince.

"He's a good boy to his mother," said one, "and she'll miss him sorely."

"He's living yet, God bless him, and perhaps after all he'll mend," declared another of more hopeful spirit.

"Did you ever hear that when he was a little chap and his tutor was going to leave him, the young man couldn't go into his room without finding a little present on his pillow or perhaps a note from the little boy saying how much he should miss him?"

"It'll kill the Queen," said one man. "The poor woman's had all she can bear, and she'll never go through this."

"And the Prince's boy's but eight years old," declared another. "There'll be a regent for ten years, and no one can say what harm will come to the country in that time."

IN THE DAYS OF QUEEN VICTORIA

So the days passed. The fourteenth of December came, the anniversary of the day on which the Prince Consort had died. The Prince breathed and that was all. The people about the offices were hushed. Everyone dreaded to hear the next message, but when it came, it said "Better." London hardly dared to rejoice, but the Prince continued to gain, and at last the Queen joyfully granted the wish of her people and appointed a Thanksgiving Day. The special service was held at St. Paul's Church, and there were many tears of joy when the Queen walked up the nave between the Prince and the Princess of Wales.

After the religious ceremony was over, the guns roared out the delight of the people, and a wild excitement of happiness began. At night St. Paul's was illuminated, and everyone was jubilant. The Queen was deeply touched and pleased with the warm sympathy shown by her subjects, and a day or two later she sent a little letter to be published in the papers to tell them how happy they had made her.

Only two days after this letter was written, there was a great alarm, for when the Queen went out to drive a young fellow sprang towards the carriage and aimed a pistol at her. He was seized in a moment and proved to be a half-crazed boy of seventeen whose pistol had neither powder nor bullet. Most of the Queen's personal attendants were Highlanders, and one of them, John Brown, had thrown himself between her and what he supposed was the bullet of an assassin. Both the Queen and Prince Albert were always most appreciative of faithful service, and looked upon it as something which money could not buy. She had been thinking of having special medals made to give to her servants who deserved a special reward, and she now gave the first one to John Brown. With the medal went an annuity of $125.

John Brown seemed to have no thought but for the Queen. To serve her and care for her was his one interest. He cared nothing about court manners, and was perhaps the only person in the land who dared to find fault with its sovereign to her face. Statesmen would bow meekly before her, but the Scotchman always spoke his mind. He even ventured to criticise her clothes. The Queen never did care very much for fine raiment, and in her journal where she narrates so minutely as to mention the fact that a glass of water was brought her, she describes her dress merely as "quite thin things." John Brown thought nothing was good enough for his royal mistress. "What's that thing ye've got on?" he would demand with most evident disapproval, if a cloak or gown was not up to his notion of what she ought to wear; and this Queen, who knew so well what was due to her position, knew also that honest affection is better than courtly manners, and kept Brown in close attendance. She built several little picnic cottages far up in the hills, where she and some of her children would often go for a few days when they were at Balmoral. There is a story that when she was staying at one of these cottages, she wished to go out to sketch. A table was brought her, but it was too high. The next was too low, and the third was not solid enough to stand firmly. So far John Brown had not interfered, but now he brought back one of the tables and said bluntly, "They canna make one for you up here." The Queen laughed and found that it would answer very well.

One cannot help wondering what Queen Victoria's guests thought of her attendant's blunt ways, but they must have often envied her his honest devotion. In 1872 and 1873 she had several very interesting visitors. One of them was David Livingstone, the African explorer.

"What do the people in the wilderness ask you?" queried the Queen.

"They ask many questions," he replied, "but perhaps the one I hear oftenest is, 'Is your Queen very rich?' and when I say 'Yes,' they ask, 'How rich is she? how many cows does she own?'"

Other visitors were a group of envoys from the King of Burmah, a monarch with such strict regard for what he looked upon as royal etiquette that he would not allow the British representative to come into his presence unless the indignant Englishman took off his shoes before attempting to enter the audience room. His letter to the Queen began with the flourishes that would be expected from so punctilious a potentate: "From His Great, Glorious, and Most Excellent Majesty, King of the Rising Sun, who reigns over Burmah, to Her Most Glorious and Excellent Majesty Victoria, Queen of Great Britain and Ireland." He sent among other gifts a gold bracelet which must have been of more value than use, for it weighed seven pounds.

The guest who made the greatest sensation was the Shah of Persia. For more than two months he was on his way to England, and the nearer he came, the more wild were the fancies that people had about him. The newspapers were full of stories about his dagger, whose diamonds were so dazzling, they said, that one might as well gaze at the midday sun. They told amazing tales about the pocket money which he had brought with him, some putting the amount as $2,500,000, others as $25,000,000. "When he walks about, jewels fall upon the ground," one newspaper declared. "He wears a black velvet tunic all sprinkled with diamonds, and he has epaulets of emeralds as big as walnuts," romanced another.

The curiosity seekers were disappointed when he appeared, though it would seem as if he had enough jewelry to make himself worth at least a glance, for up and down his coat were rows of rubies and diamonds. He wore a scimitar, and that, together with his belt and cap, was sparkling with precious stones, while his fingers were loaded with rings.

The Queen came from Balmoral to welcome him. Whether she gave him the formal kiss that was expected between sovereigns, the accounts do not state, but all sorts of entertainments were arranged for him, a great ball, a review of artillery, an Italian opera, and many other amusements. He was much interested in the review, and the troops must have been interested in him, for he rode an Arab horse whose tail had been dyed a bright pink. At this review one of the newspaper stories proved very nearly true, for a member of the Persian suite fell from his horse and really did scatter diamonds about him on the grass. After a visit of a little more than two weeks, the Shah bade farewell to England. Before his departure there was an exchange of courtesies between himself and the Queen. She made him a knight of the Garter, and he made her a member of a Persian order which he had just instituted for ladies. The Queen gave him a badge and collar of the Garter, set in diamonds; and he returned the gift by presenting her with his photograph in a circle of diamonds.

In the midst of this entertainment and display, the tender heart of the Queen was more than once deeply grieved by the death of dear friends. The cherished Féodore, the Princess Hohenlohe, died; then the Queen lost Dr. McLeod, the Scotch clergyman who had so helped and comforted her in her troubles. Hardly two months had passed after his death before heart-broken letters came from Darmstadt. Princess Alice had been away for a short time, counting the hours before she could be with her children again. At last she was at home with them and happy. The two little boys were brought to her chamber one morning, and as she stepped for a moment into the adjoining room, one of them, "Frittie," fell from the window to the stone terrace, and died in a few hours. The heart-broken mother longed to go to her own mother for comfort in her trouble, but she could not leave her home, neither could the Queen come to her.

Warm, tender words of sympathy came from England, from a Queen mother who well knew what sorrow meant. "Can you bear to play on the piano yet?" she asked some three months after the accident; for it was long after the death of Prince Albert before she herself could endure the sound of music. Princess

Alice replied, "It seems as if I never could play again on that piano, where little hands were nearly always thrust when I wanted to play. Ernie asked, 'Why can't we all die together? I don't like to die alone, like Frittie.'"

While the heart of the Queen was aching with sympathy for her daughter, she had also to attend to arrangements for the marriage of her sailor son "Affie," now Duke of Edinburgh, with the daughter of the Emperor of Russia. She herself could not go to the wedding at St. Petersburg, but she asked Dean Stanley to go and perform the English ceremony; for as the bride was a member of the Greek Church, there was a double rite. To Dean Stanley's wife she sent a mysterious little parcel containing two sprigs of myrtle, and with it a letter which asked her to put them into warm water, and when the wedding day came, to place them in a bouquet of white flowers for the bride. The myrtle had grown from the slip in the bridal bouquet of the Princess Royal, and in the five marriages of royal children that had preceded this one, each bride had carried a bit of the bush.

When the bride reached Balmoral, a company of volunteers in kilts were waiting to receive her. Just beyond were the tenants on the Queen's estate, all in their best clothes. The pipers were present, of course, and the best clothes of the Queen's pipers were well worth seeing. The kilt was of Stuart plaid, and the tunic of black velvet. Over the shoulder was a silver chain from which hung a silver powder horn. The bag for the pipe was of blue velvet. Ornaments were worn wherever there was a place for them, but the only jewels were cairngorms, and they were always set in silver. The shoes had heavy silver buckles. The bride and all her royal friends drove to the castle, where their health was drunk by a merry company. The end of the Queen's account of this reception of royalty sounds delightfully simple and homelike. "We took Marie and Alfred to their rooms downstairs," she says, "and sat with them while they had their tea."

In so large a family as that of the Queen there was always a birth or a marriage, a coming or a going. Not long after the marriage of his brother Alfred, the Prince of Wales left England to spend some months in India. This journey was not a pleasure trip, it had a state purpose, and that was to pay honor to the native princes who had aided the English in their efforts to govern India. The Prince was well accustomed to being received with cheering and the firing of guns, but his Indian reception was something entirely new. At one place twenty-four elephants painted in different colors trumpeted a greeting. In another, which was ruled by a lady, the sovereign met him, but she could hardly be said to have made her appearance, for her face was thickly veiled. At still another he was carried up a hill in a superb chair made of silver and gold. There was a boar hunt, an antelope hunt, and an elephant fight; there was a marvelously beautiful illumination of surf; there were addresses presented by people of all shades of complexion and all varieties of costume, often so magnificent that some one called the wearers "animated nuggets."

This visit of the Prince of Wales was followed by the Queen's assumption of the title of Empress of

MOTHER AND EMPRESS

India. There was a vast amount of talk about the new title, for many English thought that it was foolish and childish to make any change. On the other hand, "Empress" was the proper title for a woman who ruled over many kings, even kings of India. There were stories afloat that one reason why the Queen wished to become an Empress was because the Russian Princess, who was the daughter of an Emperor, had claimed precedence over the English Princesses, who were only the daughters of a Queen. However that may be, the title was formally assumed in 1876. It was proclaimed in India with all magnificence. Sixty-three princes were present to hear the proclamation. There were thousands of troops and long lines of elephants. A throne that was a vision of splendor was built high up above the plain; and on this sat the viceroy of the Queen, who received the honors intended for her.

Queen Victoria was much pleased with the new title, and soon began to sign her name "Victoria, R. I.," for "Regina et Imperatrix," to all documents, though it had been expected that she would affix it to her signature only when signing papers relating to India. Another title which she enjoyed was that of "Daughter of the Regiment." The Duke of Kent had been in command of the "Royal Scots" at the time of her birth and therefore they looked upon her as having been "born in the regiment." In the autumn of this same year she presented them with new colors, and there was a little ceremony which delighted her because it was evidently so sincere. There was first a salute, then marching and countermarching, while the band played old marches that were her favorites, among them one from the

"Fille du Régiment," to hint that she belonged especially to them. Then there was perfect silence. Two officers knelt before her, and she presented them with the new colors, first making a little speech. The Royal Scots were greatly pleased, because in her speech she said, "I have been associated with your regiment from my earliest infancy, and I was always taught to consider myself a soldier's child." In spite of her many years' experience in making short speeches and of her perfect calmness in public in her earlier years, the Queen was never quite at ease in speaking to an audience after Prince Albert died, and she said of this occasion, "I was terribly nervous." She never ceased to miss the supporting presence of the Prince, and she wrote pitifully of her first public appearance after his death, "There was no one to direct me and to say, as formerly, what was to be done."

The Queen was soon to feel even more lonely, for late in the autumn of 1878 there came a time of intense anxiety, then of the deepest sorrow. Princess Alice's husband and children were attacked by diphtheria. "Little Sunshine," as her youngest daughter was called in the home, died after three days' illness. The mother hid her grief as best she could that the other children should not know of their loss. Three weeks later, she too was taken with the same disease, and died on the seventeenth anniversary of her father's death. Little children and poor peasant women of Hesse were among those who laid flowers on her bier and shared in the grief of the sorrowing monarch across the Channel.

The Queen had built a cairn at Balmoral in memory of the Prince Consort. Others had been built from time to time, one rising merrily with laughing and dancing to commemorate the purchase of the estate; others erected to mark the date of the marriage of the sons and daughters of the house. To these a granite cross was now added to the memory of the beloved daughter, "By her sorrowing mother, Queen Victoria," said the inscription.

So it was that the happy circle of sons and daughters was first broken; so it was that the years of the Queen passed on, full of the joys and sorrows that seemed to come to her almost hand in hand.

CHAPTER XIV

THE JUBILEE SEASON

WITH the exception of Prince Alfred, the Queen's children had married according to the German proverb, "The oldest must leave the house first." The next in age was Prince Arthur, or the Duke of Connaught. He married in 1879 Princess Louise of Prussia with the usual magnificent display at St. George's Chapel. The real home welcome, however, was awaiting them at Balmoral, where they arrived a few months later. When the train came to a standstill, there stood the Queen and Princess Beatrice, with the Royal Scots for a guard of honor. The Queen gave the bride a bouquet of heather, and they set off for the castle. At the end of the Balmoral bridge was an arch of moss and heather with a motto in flowers, "Welcome to Balmoral." There stood the castle guests, and there were all the tenants, the women in their Sunday clothes, the men in kilts, and the pipers playing their best and loudest, while the children tossed flowers into the carriages and shouted their welcome.

Of course a cairn had been begun in honor of the marriage, and two or three days later the happy

THE JUBILEE SEASON

party went to visit it, the Queen on her pony and the others walking. There was a speech of congratulation made, and the health of the young people was drunk. "The health of the Princess Beatrice ought to be drunk," Brown declared, and that was done with so many cheers that even the dogs objected to the tumult and began to bark. After the cheering, each one of the party walked up to the cairn and laid a stone upon it. One of the stones in the foundation was already marked with the names of the Duke and Duchess and the date of their marriage.

Three years later St. George's Chapel was again ablaze with the splendor of another royal wedding, that of Prince Leopold, the eighth child of the Queen, to Princess Hélène of Waldeck-Pyrmont. In the evening a state banquet was given, and some of the guests were much amazed when, just before the Queen was to rise from the table, her two Scotch pipers in their full Highland costume appeared at the door and marched twice around the room, playing merry Scottish airs.

The home of the newly married couple was to be at Claremont, the place where the little Princess Victoria had so enjoyed herself. It had been granted to King Leopold when he married Princess Charlotte, but on his death it again became the property of the Crown. The Queen now bought it for the King's namesake. She had given to her son the title of Duke of Albany, and some of the superstitious among her subjects shook their heads at that, for so many who had borne the title had met with misfortune or even with early death.

The wedding celebrations were hardly over before the Queen's thoughts were centered upon Egypt. The Khedive of Egypt was a great borrower, and to fill his ever empty purse he had offered England some seven years previously his shares in the Suez Canal for $20,000,000. England had been very ready to buy them and also to guarantee that people who had loaned money to this spendthrift should not lose their interest. In 1882 some of the Khedive's subjects rebelled against him and got control of the government. To maintain taxation and so pay the promised interest, England must support the Khedive and put down the rebels.

The Queen hated war as badly as her predecessor Elizabeth, but as soon as she saw that it was necessary, she had no patience with delay or poor preparation. She sent directions continually to the War Office, now about arms, now about blankets or food or the comforts that would be needed in the hospitals. She never had the slightest sympathy with indecision or lack of promptness, and the moment that she thought of something that ought to be done for her soldiers, she sent a message to the Minister of War. During one day she sent him seventeen.

The troops sailed. Telegrams were frequent, and on a Monday morning in September there came to Balmoral one marked "Very secret." It was written in cipher and said, "Determined to attack the enemy with a large force on Wednesday." There could be no report of the battle for two days at least, but the Queen and her family tried hard to be brave and cheerful. More than once the Queen slipped away from them to pray

THE JUBILEE SEASON

that her son might return to her in safety, for the Duke of Connaught was in Egypt in command of a brigade. Wednesday morning a telegram came, "The army marched out last night." A second arrived a little later, "The enemy has been routed at Tel-el-Kebir, but fighting is going on." "Louischen," the wife of the Duke, was with the Queen. They could think of nothing but the husband and son, far away beside the Nile. Any moment might be the fatal one. They almost fancied they could hear the boom of the cannon. Never was a morning so long, but at last the word came, "A great victory; Duke safe and well; led his brigade to the attack." The Queen hurried to find "Louischen," and threw her arms about her neck. "How glad and proud and thankful we can be!" she exclaimed with tears, not of sorrow but of joy.

That afternoon the Duke of Albany and his wife arrived, and then there was a double rejoicing. After the drinking of healths of bride and bridegroom, John Brown stepped forward and said, "Ladies and gentlemen, let us join in a good Highland cheer for the Duke and Duchess of Albany; may they live long and die happy!" and then there was such cheering as made the woods and hills ring.

Twenty-six years before, when word had come of the fall of Sebastopol, a bonfire had been lighted on the top of Craig Gowan, and now there was another in honor of the Egyptian victory. It was very dark, but no one cared for that. The two princesses and many of the people in the house walked up to the top of the hill with the pipes playing jubilantly. There the bonfire was lighted, and the Queen watched from the windows and listened to the pipes and the cheering. When the princesses came down, they all had a little supper together "in Louischen's room."

With all these family celebrations, indeed with almost every action of the Queen's life, John Brown was closely associated. In private and in public he was the attendant of his sovereign, ever on the watch to save her, not only from danger, but from the least annoyance. On one occasion, the Queen's carriage stopped in a village after dark, and curious people thronged about. One man actually held up a lantern to get a plainer view of her face, but all that met his eyes was the rugged, determined features of John Brown, for the faithful man had calmly put himself between the Queen and her inquisitive subject. On another occasion, a woman pushed up to the carriage and stood leaning upon the wheel and staring at the Queen. John Brown thought it a waste of courtesy to be gentle with such a person, and he growled "Be off with you!" like an angry policeman to a crowd of troublesome ragamuffins. In 1883 this faithful servant died. There could hardly have been a time when the Queen had more need of him, for by a fall on the staircase at Windsor she had become unable to walk or even to stand.

During the months of her lameness, she prepared for publication a volume of extracts from her journal for 1862 to 1882. The dedication read, "To My Loyal Highlanders, and especially to the memory of my devoted personal attendant, John Brown." She was as modest about this book as about the first one, and with the copy that she presented to Tennyson she sent an almost shy little note saying, "Though a very humble and unpretending author, I send you my new book, which perhaps you may like to glance at. Its only merit is its simplicity and truth."

Windsor Castle

The Queen's lameness did not prevent her from making her usual spring visit to Balmoral in 1884, but the most unusual precautions were taken to insure her safety. Within two or three years the Emperor of Russia had been assassinated, and in London several attempts had been made recently to blow up public buildings with dynamite. Generally when the Queen traveled, her time-table was known, and people were at every station to give her welcome. An engine was always sent before the train to make sure that the road was clear, but this time, however, the time-tables were kept secret, and no spectators were allowed to gather at the stations. Men were usually at work on the road, averaging one to every half-mile. These men were now supplied with flags to wave as the train came in sight. If the engineer saw a white flag, he knew the way was clear for half a mile; but if the red one was waved, he knew there was danger or some obstruction ahead, and that he must stop at once.

The Queen was still so much of an invalid that she could stand only a few minutes when the day came that she had to be told of the sudden death of her youngest son. He was the only one of the nine children who had not been strong, but the Queen loved him all the better for his sufferings. He was much like his father in mind, and she had hoped that he would be able to act as her private secretary. Even when he was ill, he was so merry and unselfish that all who saw him loved him. He never seemed to realize that there was anything in him to call out their affection, and he once said very simply, "I can't think why people should always be so kind to me."

The Queen felt that the joy had gone from her life, but she sent to her people the message, "I will labor on as long as I can for the sake of my children and for the good of the country I love so well."

The government of her country gave her little pleasure at that time, for in spite of all that she could do, grave trouble was arising from what she believed was the mistaken course of her Ministers. Egypt had been pacified three years before, but there was revolt in the Soudan. A man named Mohammed had gone about among the wild Arabs declaring, "I am the prophet who was to follow the great Mohammed. For

THE JUBILEE SEASON

twelve hundred years the world has been awaiting me. Come and fight under my banner." Thousands rose to join him, and Mohammed, or the Mahdi, as he was called, led them against the Khedive. That ruler was helpless to repulse them. England was responsible for the good order of his country, and the Ministers debated the question long and seriously, what to do in Egypt.

"Let us send troops to the Soudan and suppress the rebellion," advised one.

"That is what the Queen wishes," said another, "but it may be that the Soudan is not worth so many lives as would be wasted in conquering the rebels."

"It is not," declared another positively. "Let us attempt nothing but to keep the Mahdi out of Egypt."

"But what of our English and Egyptian garrisons in the Soudan?" That was a grave question, and a long discussion followed. The government then in power was ready to do almost anything to avoid war. The Queen looked upon the matter differently. She was now no girl of eighteen, she was a woman with nearly fifty years' experience in dealing with nations civilized and nations uncivilized. She believed that it was best to hold on to the Soudan; but since her Ministers were determined to abandon it to the revolters, she saw that the only thing to do was to lose no time in confronting the Mahdi with an army so overwhelmingly superior to his own forces that he would not dare to attack the garrisons.

The Ministers did not agree with her. "General Gordon has already shown that he knows how to manage the people of the Soudan," they said, "and he will be able to persuade the Mahdi to let the garrisons go free."

"With an army to support him, yes," said the Queen; "but alone, no."

Nevertheless, General Gordon was sent to cross the desert almost alone. In spite of all that the brave commander could do, the Mahdi could not be persuaded to let the garrisons go, and soon the envoy himself was shut up in Khartoum. "Help us," he pleaded with England. "Send us troops." Still the government delayed, in spite of the Queen's warnings. No help came, and General Gordon then sent a messenger to beg private parties in the British colonies and the United States for money to organize a relief expedition; but the messengers were captured and put to death. The Queen urged and insisted that relief should be given, and the people insisted with her. Troops were sent at last, and they hastened on till they were only a mile and a half from Khartoum. But they were forty-eight hours too late, for the city had fallen, and General Gordon had been slain.

Queen Victoria was a constitutional monarch. She had stood firmly by her Ministers ever since the Bedchamber Plot of the first year of her reign; but she was also a woman, a loving, tender-hearted woman, and she wrote to General Gordon's sister a letter in which sympathy for her loss and indignation for the "stain left upon England" were mingled. She said:

THE JUBILEE SEASON

"Dear Miss Gordon,

"How shall I write to you, or how shall I attempt to express what I feel! To think of your dear, noble, heroic brother, who served his country and his Queen so truly, so heroically, with a self-sacrifice so edifying to the world, not having been rescued! That the promises of support were not fulfilled—which I so frequently and constantly pressed on those who asked him to go—is to me grief inexpressible."

General Gordon's diary was found and sent to his sister. Its last entry was, "I have done my best for the honor of our country. Good-by." His Bible was presented by his sister to the Queen. It was placed on a cushion of white satin in an exquisite casket of carved crystal with silver mountings. "This is one of my greatest treasures," the Queen often said, as she sadly pointed it out to her friends.

The Queen was aroused from her sorrow over what she ever looked upon as a disgrace to her country by the approaching marriage of Princess Beatrice to Prince Henry of Battenberg. Their wedding was quite different from those of the other royal children, for it was celebrated at the country church near Osborne. No one knew how to manage a royal wedding in a little village church, and there were all sorts of momentous questions to be settled before the arrangements were complete. It all came out well in the end, however. There was not room for quite so many royalties as usual, but the wedding day was a delightful holiday for the people of the Isle of Wight, for there were fireworks, bands, a dinner and a dance for all the tenants and servants on the estate, and a most beautiful display of sailing vessels and steamers. Tennyson's home was on the Isle of Wight, and the Queen sent him a charmingly informal invitation to the wedding. "It would give me the greatest pleasure," she wrote, "if you would come over for the wedding in our village church, but I fear you won't do that? But pray come and see me when all is quiet again." Tennyson did not attend the wedding, but the Princess must have counted among her choicest gifts his message, "To the royal bride the old poet sends his blessing." This marriage alone of all those in the royal family was not to bring separation, for it was agreed that the Princess and Prince Henry should remain with the Queen.

This Queen and Empress had now been on the throne for nearly half a century, and throughout her dominions there was a feeling that so rare an event ought to be celebrated with fitting magnificence. The Jubilee feeling was in the air. Every town and every little village wished to mark the time by something that should remain as a lasting memorial. Libraries, hospitals, and museums were founded, and parks were purchased and thrown open to the public. Memorial clocks, statues, schools, and towers sprang into being in every corner of the land, and in all the colonies. "God Save the Queen" was sung in Hindustanee on the shores of Asia and in Hebrew in the synagogues of London. Addresses of congratulation and loyalty came in by the score; representatives of all the colonies flocked to England, as sons and daughters hastened homeward to a family gathering.

THE JUBILEE SEASON

The part to be taken in the celebration by associations, cities, and kingdoms had all been planned when it occurred to the editor of one of the London newspapers that nobody had remembered the children. "Let us give the boys and girls of London a feast and an entertainment in Hyde Park," he suggested. "You can't do it," declared the grumblers. "It is a foolish, wicked scheme. There will be a crush, accidents will happen, and hundreds will be injured." Nevertheless, people subscribed so generously that soon all the money needed had been provided. When the children came to the Park, they were taken in groups to great tents; and when they came out, each one had a paper bag which contained "a meat pie, a piece of cake, a bun, and an orange." Their little hands must have been full, for besides the eatables, each one received a little medallion portrait of the Queen and a Jubilee mug. The mugs saw hard service among the thirsty little folk, for all day milk, lemonade, and ginger beer were free to every child who presented his empty mug. The children were amused by all sorts of games and shows. Dukes and princes and representatives of powerful kingdoms came to see the good time; and at last the Queen herself came and gave a special greeting, not to the grown folk, but every word of it to the children. Long before bedtime had come, every one of the twenty-seven thousand small people was safe in his own home, and the grumblers grumbled no more.

June 21, 1887, was "Jubilee Day." Fifty years had passed since the young girl had been aroused from her sleep to hear that she was Queen of a mighty nation; and now, in all the glory of her half century of successful sovereignty, she was to go to Westminster Abbey to thank God for his help and protection.

She now represented, not a kingdom, but an enormous empire, and every corner of it wished to do her honor. The streets of London were spanned by triumphal arches. They were made into a fairyland of flowers, banners, drapings of silk and velvet and tapestry. Staging for seats had been put up all along the route, and every seat was filled. Fabulous prices were paid for a house, a window or even a few square inches on a rough plank. Thousands of people had been out since sunrise to secure a place to see the grand procession; and at last it came in sight, moving slowly toward the multitude that waited all a-tremble with excitement and with devotion to the noble woman who was the symbol of home and country.

First came the carriages containing the dark-faced princes of India, robed in cloth of gold, and shaded with turbans glittering with priceless jewels. Many carriages followed, filled with kings, queens, crown princes, and grand dukes. There were equerries, aides-de-camp, an escort of Life Guards, and a guard of honor composed of princes riding three abreast, the Queen's sons, grandsons, sons-in-law and grandsons-in-law. Towering up among them was the superb figure of Prince "Fritz," Crown Prince of a united Germany. His uniform was of pure white, his helmet of burnished steel, and on it was the Prussian eagle with outspread wings. At last the woman for whom all were waiting came in sight. The splendid robes of her coronation were fifty years behind her, but even in her plainer dress she looked every inch a queen. The Prin-

THE JUBILEE SEASON

cess Alexandra and the Crown Princess of Germany were with her. For twenty-five years the sovereign had so rarely appeared in public that to her subjects this was more than a mere royal procession, it was the coming back to them of their Queen. A great wave of devotion and loyalty swept over the hearts of the throng. "Not *the* Queen, but *my* Queen," they said to themselves, and such a greeting was given her as few monarchs have received.

The Abbey had been filled long before. Rich strains of music were coming from the organ. There was a moment's silence, then the silver trumpets of the heralds were blown, and the church resounded with Handel's march from the "Occasional Oratorio." The Queen entered. She was preceded by archbishops, bishops, and deans, all in the most elaborate vestments of their offices. The guard of royal princes walked slowly up the nave, three abreast, the Prince of Wales and his two brothers coming last. Slowly the Queen to whom all the world was doing honor, ascended the steps of the throne. The vast assemblage was hushed, and stood for a moment with heads bowed in reverence.

A short, simple service followed of praise and thanksgiving. Then her sons and daughters, who had been grouped around the Queen, came forward one at a time to bow before her and kiss her hand. As they rose, she gave each of them a kiss, not of state, but of warm, motherly affection that in this crowning moment of her career could not be satisfied with the restrictions of ceremony.

That evening there were fireworks and illuminations in all the principal cities. England shone literally from shore to shore, for a beacon fire was lighted on Malvern Hills, and in a moment, as its distant gleam shone on other hills, other beacons blazed, till from Land's End to the Shetland Islands it was rejoicingly written in letters of fire that for fifty years the realm had been under the rule of a pure and upright womanhood.

At last the day was fully ended. "I am very happy," said the Queen; and well she might be, for this day had shown her that she was sovereign, not only of the land and its treasures, but of the loving hearts of her subjects.

CHAPTER XV

THE QUEEN AND THE CHILDREN

THERE had been only one drawback to the Queen's happiness during the Jubilee rejoicings, and that was the poor health of her favorite son-in-law, the Crown Prince of Germany. In the procession he had looked superbly well and strong, but his throat was giving him so much trouble that he remained in England the rest of the year, hoping that a change of climate would do him good.

Everyone loved "Our Fritz," as he was called in Germany, both his own countrymen and the English. His father, the Emperor, was over ninety and so feeble that he could not possibly live many months. Ever since that summer day on the hills of Balmoral when the Prince had given the sprig of white heather to the maiden of his choice, the Queen had hoped that Germany would unite under one emperor and that Prince Frederick William would become its ruler. The German states had united, and it was clear that the German throne would soon fall to her daughter's husband; but the physicians declared that his disease was incurable.

IN THE DAYS OF QUEEN VICTORIA

For several months the whole world watched for news of the beloved Emperor and his equally beloved son. Early in 1888 the Emperor died, and Queen Victoria's ambition of thirty years had come to pass; her daughter was Empress of Germany. But it was a sad accession to a throne, and the Queen forgot all about her ambitious hopes in her daughter's grief and her own. Hardly a day passed that she did not send some message of sympathy to the sorrowing wife. In three months the end came. The Emperor "Fritz," whose sufferings had been none the less because he sat on a throne, was dead. His son, the Frederick William Victor Albert who had given his young uncles so much trouble at the wedding of the Prince of Wales, now wore the German crown; but the Queen, instead of rejoicing in her daughter's being Empress of Germany, could only try as best she might to help her bear her loneliness.

No one, whether Princess Royal or Highland cottager, ever appealed to the Queen for sympathy in vain. She was always especially interested in the sick. In her Jubilee year, the women of England made her a present of $375,000, and she gave almost all of it to found an institute which should provide trained nurses for the poor in their own homes. When injured soldiers returned to England, she was never weary of going to see them, of walking down the long rows of beds, saying to one man, "I am afraid you are in great pain," to another, "England owes much to her brave soldiers." If she only asked "Where were you wounded?" or looked at a sufferer with that peculiarly sweet smile of which everyone spoke and which the photographers could never catch, he was content. Some of the hospital patients almost believed that her coming would cure them.

"Oh, it does hurt so," sobbed one little girl in a ward for children, "but if the Queen would only come and see me, I know I'd be well."

"Perhaps she will," said the nurse.

"No," cried the little one. "She went right by the door."

Somehow word was carried to the Queen that a little girl who had been terribly burned was crying to see her.

"Is there another ward that I have not visited?" she asked.

"Yes, Madam," answered the Doctor, "but it is at the extreme end of the hospital."

"Never mind," replied the Queen. "I will go and see the child."

After this visit the little girl who had been so honored was the envy of all the other children as she told over and over her story of the royal visit. "She came down just to see me," said the little one, "the Doctor told me she did. She put her hand right on my forehead and she said, 'I have a little granddaughter about as old as you, and I hope you will soon be able to run about as she does.' And then she said 'Good-by,' and she said, 'I shall come to see you again.' I wish she would come to-morrow."

IN THE DAYS OF QUEEN VICTORIA

All her life Queen Victoria was fond of children. She liked even the little boy who declared stoutly, "No, I don't like you because you cut Mary Queen of Scots' head off." When she first became Queen, she always managed to have some little folks staying in the palace as visitors, and the ninth child of her own family was just as welcome as the first. In all the displays that were made at her various receptions, she was never more pleased than when throngs of children were gathered together to greet her. She knew how to please children, and when she went to visit a school for boys, she won their hearts by requesting the master to give them an extra week's holiday. She never could bear to disappoint a child. One day when she was driving very rapidly, she caught sight of a little boy by the roadside looking much grieved because he had tried to throw a bunch of flowers into her carriage, and it had fallen into the road. "Drive back," she ordered, and the carriage with its four horses and driver and attendants was turned back. "Will you give me those pretty flowers?" she asked, and the little boy with tears on his cheeks suddenly became the happiest little fellow in the Highlands, as he shyly handed her the rather dusty bouquet. The children of the Balmoral tenants knew that she would never forget her promises, and if she said a toy was coming to them at Christmas, it was as sure to come as the day itself. When the little daughter of the minister in the village nearest to Balmoral was born, the Queen asked that she might be named Alexandrina Victoria for herself. Many gifts were sent to the little namesake, but perhaps the one that pleased her most was the tall sugar ornament from the Queen's birthday

THE QUEEN AND THE CHILDREN

cake which the Queen herself brought over to the home of the tiny damsel and presented to her.

As the many grandchildren began to circle around Queen Victoria, she had a warm corner in her heart for everyone. She always wore a bracelet with a place for a miniature, and here the picture of the "new baby" was put, to remain until there was a newer baby whose little portrait should take its place. The numerous grandchildren and great-grandchildren were taught to greet her with the utmost respect, and little boys who could hardly walk would make a bow to her or kiss her hand as gravely as any grown-up courtiers. There the ceremony ended, and the good times began.

Of all the groups of children there were some to whom she was especially devoted. The daughters of the Princess Alice, as she was always called in England, she cared for almost as if they were her own. They made her long and frequent visits, and, little as the Queen cared for handsome clothes, she saw to it that when these orphan granddaughters were to be married, they should have all sorts of fine apparel and many beautiful jewels.

The children of whom she saw most during the last years of her life were those of Princess Beatrice. Two of them were born at Balmoral, first, a little Victoria Eugénie, the first child of the royal family born in Scotland for three hundred years. The tenants felt that this child was really their own, and they put their shillings together and bought her a very handsome cradle. They were all invited to come to the castle and see the baby, and a carriage was sent for any who were too feeble to walk. When the second child, a boy, was born, Craig Gowan again blazed with a bonfire. The pipers played, and all the people on the estate lighted their torches and marched up to the top of the hill for a dance.

It is to be hoped that the Princess Beatrice did not have as much difficulty in managing her own children as she did when she was six years old in commanding the obedience of Prince Frederick William of Germany and his sister. She is said to have gone to Dr. McLeod, declaring indignantly, "Just think, my nephew William and my niece Elizabeth will not do as I bid them and shut the door, and I am their aunt! Aren't they naughty?"

One little grandchild who was especially dear to the Queen was the son of her son Leopold, who died so suddenly. The Duke of Albany commanded the "Seaforth Highlanders," and after his death the little Duke was looked upon as their commander. The story is told that when he was six years old, he was allowed to "review" his troops. Very seriously he set about it, wearing a uniform made just like that of the tall Highlanders. He had been carefully taught how to give some of the orders, and he piped them out as gravely as if the fate of a battle depended upon his words. He was delighted to see how promptly the men obeyed him, and he felt quite like a grown man; but he too had to obey as implicitly as his soldiers, and when he made a boat of a scrubbing brush belonging to a tenant, and it floated off down the river, the small boy was taken straightway to a village store to buy another and pay for it with his own pocket money.

THE QUEEN AND THE CHILDREN

With so many children in whom she was interested, the Queen might well have been forgiven if she had forgotten a few of them at Christmas, but such a thing never occurred; and even when the birthdays came around, they were never overlooked. She always had a little pity for her own lonely childhood, and she was very fond of giving her children and grandchildren feasts and entertainments that they could enjoy together. Dancing bears were brought to Windsor to perform for the children; Punch and Judy often gave them a merry hour; and once at least a monkey was "commanded" to appear before the Queen with his owner and the hand-organ. Where other people "invited," the Queen "commanded." Performers were very ready to obey, for besides the price paid them by the palace commissioner, the Queen almost always made them a personal gift of money or jewelry. Moreover, it was an excellent advertisement for them to perform before the royal family. Among other performers Buffalo Bill and his troupe were commanded to Windsor to show her Majesty and the little people what wild life on the plains of America used to be.

Once at Balmoral the Queen commanded a circus to perform before her. It was only a little circus, and the proprietor must have been almost overwhelmed with amazement and delight, but he made ready and set out for a field near the castle. The "Battenberg children" and the little folk from the other two castles which the Queen had built near Balmoral were summoned to come to the show. The little Alexandrina Victoria was invited, and word was sent to all the tenant children. The circus began. The children were happy, and even the performing donkey did so finely that the Queen wished to buy him. Unfortunately he was only a borrowed donkey and could not be sold; but after this fortunate day, it is very likely that whenever he entered the sawdust ring, he was announced as "Donkey in Special to Her Majesty the Queen of Great Britain and Ireland and Empress of India."

The Queen was never bored by these little entertainments, for with all her dignity, she had, as her husband said of his eldest daughter, "the brain of a statesman and the heart of a child." When the circus came to Balmoral, she watched it for two long hours, and was apparently as much amused as her small grandchildren; and when the organ-grinder and his monkey were at Windsor, the Queen laughed as heartily as any of the children as the little creature tried his best to find a way into the castle.

When the Queen was amused, she was very much amused, and sometimes she found it as hard to keep from laughing outright as any young girl. One who was present describes the reception of an embassy from one of the Oriental countries when it was all the Queen could do to "keep a straight face." On the English side everything was very ceremonious, for it was desirable to pay special courtesy to the strangers. The embassy, too, wished to show extreme respect, but no one guessed how they would do it. They entered, and after making all sorts of strange gestures, they "suddenly bowed themselves, apparently as men struggling with acute internal pain, and squeezed their hands together between their knees." The Queen was as motionless as a statue, her face becoming more and more grave as the formalities proceeded. The moment the envoys had left the room, however, she broke down and laughed till her eyes were full of tears. "But I went through it," she cried to her ladies. "I did go right through it."

The Queen was no less kind to her servants than to children; but just as her children were taught to obey her, so her servants were required to give her prompt and excellent service. "I can't afford to be kept waiting," she would say, whether the delinquent was a servant or a court lady. "If I am to get through my work, I mustn't have my moments frittered away." After the housekeeping was once fully in her own hands, there was little more of the irregular, negligent management that had formerly prevailed. Everyone employed had his work and was responsible for its being well done. It is said that she even made use of the ancient expedient of housekeepers whose dusting has not been properly done, and that with her own royal forefinger she once wrote her name on a dusty cabinet. The next day the dust was still there, and then she wrote under her own name that of the servant who was in fault. When the poor girl discovered that she had been reproved by the Queen of Great Britain and Empress of India, she was so overwhelmed with alarm that she ran away. It is a pleasant ending to the story to know that the royal mistress sent for her to come back. The Queen's rule was very strict, but if trouble came to any of her attendants, she was as sympathetic as if she had been one of their own family. She wanted them to have plenty of amusement, and when in 1886 a great exhibition was going on in London, she gave to her

Balmoral servants an invitation to spend ten days at Windsor Castle to see the exhibition and the other sights of the city. The Queen demanded the best of service, but when it was given, she never felt that money alone would pay for it, and she was honestly grateful to those who served her well. She had to meet so many strangers that it was a pleasure to her to have familiar faces in her household. When new attendants were to be employed, she was always glad to have members of the families that already served her; and at the death of John Brown, she gave his place to one of his cousins, who was already in her employ. When her servants were ill or unable to work, she always cared for them, and saw to it that they had a comfortable home for their old age.

The life of the Queen was gradually becoming very regular in some respects, and especially in the way that she divided her year. For a long time she had made two visits to Balmoral each year, one in the spring and one in the autumn. She made also three visits to Osborne and spent a week or more in London. The rest of her time was given to Windsor and to her "vacation," which she spent somewhere on the Continent. It is hardly fair to say that she had a vacation, for wherever she went, one of her Ministers accompanied her and the ever-present dispatch boxes followed her. At Balmoral the "Queen's Messenger" arrived about six o'clock every morning with his box of papers. These were arranged by the secretary in such a way as to save her all unnecessary trouble. About ten, she entered upon the government business of the day, reading, thinking, signing papers, and writing. At half-past two the messenger set out for London.

But this was not all her work with the pen, for the royal family carried on a vast amount of correspondence with the Queen. As nearly as possible, she wished to hear from each one of them every day, not the kind of letter that says, "I am well and hope you are the same," but letters that told what the writers were doing, and what they thought of the events in which they took part. The Queen could not answer all these communications, of course, but if there was need of her advice or sympathy, she never failed to write; and those of her letters that have been made public are charmingly frank and sincere and full of most tender affection.

Her own marriage had been so happy that in the marriage of her descendants she paid little attention to whether a proposed alliance would be of advantage to the kingdom; the chief question in her mind was whether the young people would be happy together. Two years after the Jubilee, the eldest daughter of the Prince of Wales married the Duke of Fife. According to English custom, the daughter of a Prince is not a peer, but a commoner, and although a title is usually given her, it is only by courtesy and not by right. The Princess Louise, then, was a commoner, but by marrying a Duke she became a duchess, and would have the right to precede her sisters if they did not also marry dukes or men of higher rank. One other privilege that she acquired was that, if she was accused of any crime, she could demand to be tried by a jury composed of peers.

IN THE DAYS OF QUEEN VICTORIA

In 1891 came the fiftieth anniversary of Queen Victoria's marriage, her "Golden Wedding," as her children tenderly called the day. They gave her a prayer book in which was written a stanza given them by Tennyson:

> "Remembering him who waits thee far away,
> And with thee, Mother, taught us first to pray,
> Accept on this, your golden bridal day,
> The Book of Prayer."

Through the sorrowful memories that thoughts of her own wedding aroused, the Queen was looking forward with much pleasure to a marriage that she hoped would take place. Next to the sovereign herself and the Prince of Wales, the interest of the English centered upon "Prince Eddie," the Duke of Clarence and Avondale, for after his father, he would wear the English crown, and the whole country was waiting to see whom he would choose for his wife. Princess Mary of Cambridge, who had always been a warm friend of Princess Alexandra, had married the Duke of Teck. Their daughter Mary was the choice of the Duke of Clarence, and late in 1891 the engagement was announced. Only a month passed before the Duke was taken ill, and in a few days he died. There was a deep and general mourning, for "Prince Eddie" was greatly loved; but to the Queen there was the loss not only of the first child of her first-born son, but of the heir to her crown. She wrote to Tennyson, "Was there ever a more terrible contrast, a wedding with bright hopes turned into a funeral?"

THE QUEEN AND THE CHILDREN

The English people grieved for the loss of "Prince Eddie," whom Tennyson called "so princely, tender, truthful, reverent, pure," and they were sad for the young Princess, "Princess May," as she was always called, for her merry disposition and good heart had made her a general favorite. She said of herself that when she was a child, she was "very naughty, very happy, and very uninteresting," but the people who knew her did not agree that she was either naughty or uninteresting. She and the children of the Prince of Wales were old playfellows and the best of friends. Time passed on, and it began to be whispered that a marriage would take place between Princess May and Prince George, the second son of the Prince of Wales. He was now the heir to the throne, and the people were glad that Princess May would some day become their Queen.

Prince George, or the Duke of York, had spent some years of his life at sea, for before he was twelve years old he entered the navy. The other midshipmen were on the watch to see whether he would put on airs because he was the Prince of Wales's son, but he soon showed himself ready to take part in whatever came up, and no more favor was shown him than to any other young sailor. Like his uncle, the Duke of Edinburgh, he was called the Sailor Prince. After his marriage to Princess May had taken place, and the young pair were on their way to Sandringham, they found arches built over the road, and on one was "God bless our Sailor Prince."

A loss which in her daily life touched the Queen even more nearly than that of the Duke of Clarence, was that of Prince Henry of Battenberg. In 1895 the Africans of Ashanti revolted against British rule, and forces were sent to suppress them. Prince Henry wished to serve. "I have been brought up as a soldier," he said, "and now is my time to show what I can do." The Queen was not willing to have him go, but he did not give up. "England is my adopted country," he urged. "I belong to her regular army, and I ought to help protect her interests; and for the sake of my children I ought to establish my position." Even the Princess Beatrice could not deny that this was true, and at last the Queen yielded. The service of the Prince was short, for not many weeks after reaching Africa, he was sent home ill of fever, and died on the voyage. The Queen suffered with her daughter, for the bright, merry ways of the Prince had been a real delight to her. "I have lost the sunbeam of my household," she said sadly. One by one she was losing those who were dear to her, but in every trouble the love of her subjects was her great comfort, and this love was soon to be manifested even more clearly than at the Jubilee of 1887.

CHAPTER XVI

THE CLOSING YEARS

ONE autumn day in 1896 vast numbers of telegrams were sent to Queen Victoria, not only from the English colonies, but from almost all the countries of the world. They were full of congratulations on the length of her reign; for now she had been on the throne longer than any other English ruler, and longer than any one who had ever ruled on the Continent except Louis XIV. No European monarch who had been on the throne at her accession or even ten years after her accession was still reigning. She had seen change of government, assassination, revolution, in other kingdoms, but the monarchy in England had stood firm and was much stronger than when she became Queen.

England would not permit such an event as this to pass without a celebration. Preparations for the "Diamond Jubilee" to mark Victoria's sixty years of sovereignty were commenced many months before the time appointed. More than a million strangers were expected to be in London during the two weeks of the festivities, and the hotel-keepers began to plan how to feed them. Non-perishable foods were brought thousands of miles, and fields of vegetables were bought before they were planted. Next to something to eat, the visitors would wish for a place to see, and owners of houses standing on the route to be taken by the procession expected to get more for a single window than the usual rent of a house for a year. The tenants of these houses were given notice to quit, and as the time drew near, those who refused to leave were put out by force. These removals were called "Jubilee Evictions."

Not everybody was busy with plans for money-making. There was an enormous amount of decorating going on. "V. R." was everywhere and in all sorts of materials, from cut glass and gold to red calico. There were roses, lions, crowns, unicorns, wreaths, banners, and pictures of the Queen at every turn. The route which the procession was to follow wound past the homes of the poor as well as those of the rich, and even the poorest found means to brighten the dingiest abode with a bit of color.

As June 22, 1897, drew near, troops from every British colony began to be seen in the streets of London. Uniforms of red, white, yellow, brown, green, blue, and all kinds of minglings and mixtures decorated the city. There were so many Chinese, Africans, and Hindus, brown people, yellow people, and white people, from every part of the world, that one might almost wonder whether there would be room in the streets for the Londoners, if they should attempt to leave their homes. It looked as if it might be a little difficult to leave some of the houses, for scaffoldings had been built in front of them, and sometimes even far

THE CLOSING YEARS

above the roofs, so that as many seats as possible might be rented. The procession was to follow a route six miles long, and so many high scaffolds had been raised that the march would be like a journey through a canyon whose sides were all aglow with every kind of decoration that could be imagined; for the people seemed to feel that the brighter their hangings were, the more loyal they were showing themselves to be, and the result was gorgeous if not always beautiful.

In the colonies the day was being celebrated, and telegrams of loyalty and congratulation were coming to the Queen by the score. As she passed through the doors of Buckingham Palace at eleven o'clock, she sent to every colony the message: "From my heart I thank you, my beloved people. May God bless you." Then she entered her carriage and passed on, escorted by kings, princes, long lines of seamen, masses of British troops and masses of colonial troops. The long cavalcade went on slowly to Temple Bar, the old entrance to the city. There the Queen paused, and the thousands in line paused. The Mayor, most imposing in his long velvet cloak, presented her with the sword of London in token of the city's homage. She touched the sword in acceptance, and the procession moved on.

The second stop was at St. Paul's. The eight cream-colored horses were reined up before a superb mass of color and glitter, for on the steps of the church were ambassadors, bishops, archbishops, judges, and musicians, flashing with diamonds, gleaming in cloth of gold, gorgeous in the red, blue, and pink hoods of the universities, and all framing in a great square of white-robed little choir-boys. Prayer was offered, the Te Deum was chanted, "God Save the Queen" was sung, and thousands of people wiped their eyes as they joined in "Praise God from whom all blessings flow." The benediction was pronounced, and the procession turned slowly away. And as the tread of the horses sounded again on the pavement, the Archbishop forgot his magnificent canonicals, he forgot everything except that he was an Englishman and that Victoria was his Queen, and he led the whole ten thousand people in three tremendous cheers for their sovereign.

That night everything was illuminated that could be illuminated; and, as in 1887, beacon fires flashed from hill to hill and from headland to headland. The Prince of Wales suggested that the best memorial of the day would be a general subscription to pay the debts of the principal hospitals, and in a great sweep of generosity $3,750,000 was promptly subscribed. The Princess of Wales wrote to the Lord Mayor of London, expressing her interest in the poor of the city, and gifts amounting to $1,500,000 were made at once for their benefit. The rejoicing went on for a fortnight. There were reviews of soldiers and of battleships, there were concerts, exhibitions, and dinners for the poor. One part of the celebration was the manufacture of a mammoth cake by the same firm that made the coronation cake. This Jubilee cake weighed five hundred pounds, and five hundred more were added to it in frosting and sugar ornaments. Around it was a great wreath of sugar roses. A lofty tower of sugar rose from within the wreath with many monograms, medallions,

THE CLOSING YEARS

crowns, lions, unicorns, angels of fame and of glory blowing great sugar trumpets; and at the very top was the angel of Peace with white and shining wings.

It would have been a source of deep happiness to the Queen if peace could have prevailed throughout the empire during those last years of her life, but in 1899 war arose between the English and the Boers of South Africa. As usual, she hoped to the last that there would be no war, but when she saw that it must come, she had no patience with the least delay in sending troops, and she urged re-enforcing the army so that the war might be ended as soon as possible. She was not satisfied with acting through others; she wanted to do something for the men herself with her own hands, and she set to work to knit caps and comforters to be sent them. When Christmas came, she distributed toys and candy among the soldiers' children; and, remembering that "Men are only boys grown tall," she sent 100,000 boxes of chocolate to her soldiers at the front. When the wounded and the ill were brought home, she often went to the hospitals, and she had many convalescents come to visit her at Windsor.

In this African war the Irish troops had shown such bravery that the heart of the Queen was completely won. She said to her Ministers:

"I have decided to pay a visit to Ireland to thank those brave Irishmen."

The Ministers were delighted to have her make the visit, but they remembered that she had not been in Ireland for forty years and that the Irish felt they had little reason to love the English government. "It will be only wise to have an escort of cavalry around your carriage," they suggested.

"No," she answered. "I am their Queen, and they are my people. If I showed any distrust of them, they would think I deserved to be afraid of them."

Punch published a picture of Hibernia kissing the hand of the sovereign and saying: "Sure, your Majesty, there's no place like home, and it's at home you'll be with us."

The Queen was right in trusting herself without fear to the people of Ireland; for however they might feel toward the English government, they would show nothing but respect to the English Queen who had made herself the guest of their country.

She landed at Kingstown and was received with all due form by the Lord Lieutenant of Ireland; but the more ceremonious reception was awaiting her at Dublin, where elaborate preparations had been made. The Lord Mayor and the other officials of the city were all in their long red robes heavily trimmed with fur. Attendants in black velvet and silver lace followed them, one holding a great basket of flowers high up, so that all the people could see it. A table, richly draped with silk, was placed before the Mayor. On the table was a blue satin cushion, and on the cushion was a golden casket. The casket was lined with pearl-colored silk strewn with shamrocks embroidered in blue, and in the casket were the keys of the city, and an address to the sovereign.

THE CLOSING YEARS

Of course these were not real keys of a real gate, for Dublin has no gates, but in order to carry out the interesting old ceremony, tall gates and towers of painted canvas had been erected, and as the Queen and her escort drew near, a trumpeter from the highest watchtower blew three resounding blasts and cried:

"The Athlone pursuivant is at the gates."

"With what message does he come?" asked the Lord Mayor.

"He is the bearer of a request from the Queen of Great Britain and Ireland," replied the trumpeter.

"He may enter."

The pursuivant entered, and the Lord Mayor demanded:

"With what message do you come to the gates of the city of Dublin?"

"I bear the request of the Queen of Great Britain and Ireland that she may enter her city of Dublin," he replied.

"Open the gates and admit the Queen of Great Britain and Ireland," commanded the Lord Mayor.

The pursuivant galloped back; the gates were flung wide open; the Household Cavalry dashed through; and then came the Queen. The Lord Mayor presented the beautiful casket and made his address; the Queen handed him a written reply; the Lady Mayoress presented the basket of flowers; and the Queen had been formally received as the guest of the nation.

IN THE DAYS OF QUEEN VICTORIA

This three-weeks' visit to Ireland was one of the Queen's "vacations," but it was hardly a restful time, for she visited hospitals, orphan asylums, schools, and convents; she received delegations of nurses and doctors, and entertained the prominent people of the country. She went to the Zoölogical Gardens and made the acquaintance of a baby bear, and two baby lions, who were just as cross as if she had not been their lawful sovereign. She took drives about the city and the country; she reviewed troops; and finally she accepted an invitation to review thirty thousand school children. In this review, she was much amused when one small child called out, "Sure, you're a nice old lady!" One school was delayed, but in order not to disappoint the children, the Queen arranged a little reception for them later in the day.

The visit to Ireland had given the Queen pleasure, but the continued fighting with the Boers was a grief to her, and in the summer of 1900 she had to meet trouble that touched her even more nearly in the death of her son Alfred, Duke of Connaught. The Duchy of Saxe-Coburg-Gotha had asked him to become its ruler, and the Duke of Albany had been appointed his successor. This Duke of Albany, who had reviewed his regiment of Highlanders when he was six years of age, was now sixteen, and in two years more he would sit on a throne.

So the years of the Queen passed on with their joys and sorrows. Her visit to Ireland took place in 1900. For four or five years previous to this date she had suffered so much from rheumatism that it was hard for her to walk, and in the house she was gener-

THE CLOSING YEARS

ally moved about in a wheeled chair. The door of her special car was widened so that the chair could be taken in easily. Two years before going to Ireland, her eyes began to trouble her. "Use black ink and a broad pen" were the instructions she gave to her Ministers; but even though her sight grew faint, she would not lay down the task that she felt was her own.

Toward the end of 1900 she seemed less strong than usual. "You must save yourself in every possible way," ordered the physicians, "and you must not write more than is absolutely necessary." Christmas was near, but this year her greetings to each member of her family were written for her. Letters and telegrams were read to her, but her interest in all matters was as strong as ever, and her judgments were as rapid and sagacious. She met Lord Roberts on his return from South Africa and questioned him closely about all the details of the war. Two or three days later, when she awoke in the morning, she seemed very weak, and her speech was less clear than usual. Telegrams were sent to the members of her family. Germany was in the midst of an enthusiastic celebration of the two hundredth anniversary of the establishment of the Prussian monarchy; but Emperor William said: "It is my sorrow and my nation's sorrow. Let the festivities cease." He left his kingdom and hastened to England. On the day after his arrival, January 22, 1901, Queen Victoria, with her children and grandchildren about her, passed quietly away.

The Queen had never liked the gloomy trappings of funerals, and long before this she had bidden that about her own there should be no touch of the somber and sorrowful. The room in which she lay was hung with deep red. There were palms and flowers around it, and about the bier were many tall white candles. The ermine-lined robe of the Garter was laid upon her coffin together with the flag of the country that she had loved. Grenadiers stood motionless, two at the head and two at the foot, keeping guard about her with bowed heads and arms reversed.

Osborne House, Isle of Wight.
Where Queen Victoria died, January 22nd, 1901

So she lay in her own home at Osborne until the day of the funeral was come. No hearse was driven to her door, for the soldier's gun-carriage was to bear the soldier's daughter to her resting place. The bier was covered with ruby velvet. Over it was thrown a pall of white satin with heavy edge of gold and the royal arms in each corner. On this was laid the royal standard, the crown, the insignia of the Garter, and the golden orb of empire which she had carried in her hand at her coronation. In white and gold, the emblems of purity and royalty, she went forth from her home for the last time. Her children and grandchildren, princes and princesses, walked slowly behind her down the long avenue of trees, whose branches shown out clear and distinct against the bright blue of the sky. At the water's edge, the gun-carriage, was drawn on board the yacht *Alberta*. Followed by the *Victoria and Albert*, the *Osborne*, and the massive *Hohenzollern* of the Emperor William, the little yacht moved through the mighty lines of war-ships, English, German, and French, whose cannon thundered out their last salute.

This was the farewell of the navy. That night the yacht with its precious burden lay quietly in harbor; and in the morning the body of the Queen was placed on the train to be carried to London. There houses that so lately had been all aglow with the colors of gladness were now draped with purple and white. Throngs were in the streets, but they stood in perfect silence, the men bareheaded, and every woman with some badge of mourning. Slowly the gun-carriage was drawn through the city, followed first by the two sons of the Queen with the German Emperor, then by her other relatives, by members of the royal family in Europe, and troops representing every branch of the army. The navy was also present in a guard of honor of sailors, and it was they who were called upon to perform a last service for their Queen. At Windsor the horses of the gun-carriage had become uneasy, and in a moment, with hardly a word of command, they were unharnessed, and the sailors themselves drew the gun-carriage to the castle. That afternoon the funeral rites were observed in St. George's Chapel with words of prayer and the strains of music that the Queen herself had chosen. The herald made solemn proclamation that Queen Victoria was dead and that her oldest son, Edward VII., was King of Great Britain and Ireland and Emperor of India.

On the following morning the body of the Queen was borne to the beautiful mausoleum at Frogmore which she had erected for Prince Albert nearly forty years before. Muffled drums were beaten; sad, sweet funeral marches were played by the martial bands; and so, through the long avenues lined with soldiers, the procession moved onward. At Frogmore, the bands were hushed, and the Highland pipers, walking before the coffin, played the weird, mournful strains of the "Lament of the Black Watch." Prayer was said, earth from the Mount of Olives was dropped softly upon the coffin, and the Queen was laid to rest beside her beloved Prince.

Next morning the flowers were faded, the flags were no longer at half-mast, the stores and offices were opened, and life went on as before; but in the homes of England those who had known and loved the Queen were talking of her tenderly and thoughtfully. "She always did what she believed was right," said some. "She was always sorry for those who suffered," said others; and some repeated reverently the words of the Scottish pastor who had known her so well:

"I admire her as a woman, love her as a friend, and reverence her as a Queen."